At Issue

| The Alaska Gas Pipeline

Other Books in the At Issue Series:

At Issue

I The Alaska Gas Pipeline

Stefan Kiesbye, Book Editor

GREENHAVEN PRESS
A part of Gale, Cengage Learning

GALE
CENGAGE Learning™

Detroit • New York • San Francisco • New Haven, Conn • Waterville, Maine • London

GALE
CENGAGE Learning·

Christine Nasso, *Publisher*
Elizabeth Des Chenes, *Managing Editor*

© 2010 Greenhaven Press, a part of Gale, Cengage Learning.

For more information, contact:
Greenhaven Press
27500 Drake Rd.
Farmington Hills, MI 48331-3535
Or you can visit our Internet site at gale.cengage.com

For product information and technology assistance, contact us at

Gale Customer Support, 1-800-877-4253
For permission to use material from this text or product, submit all requests online at www.cengage.com/permissions

Further permissions questions can be e-mailed to permissionrequest@cengage.com

Articles in Greenhaven Press anthologies are often edited for length to meet page requirements. In addition, original titles of these works are changed to clearly present the main thesis and to explicitly indicate the author's opinion. Every effort is made to ensure that Greenhaven Press accurately reflects the original intent of the authors. Every effort has been made to trace the owners of copyrighted material.

LIBRARY OF CONGRESS CATALOGING-IN-PUBLICATION DATA

The Alaska Gas Pipeline / Stefan Kiesbye, book editor.
    p. cm. -- (At issue)
    Includes bibliographical references and index.
    ISBN 978-0-7377-4864-2 (hardcover) -- ISBN 978-0-7377-4865-9 (pbk.)
    1. Natural gas pipelines--Alaska--Juvenile literature. 2. Natural gas--Transportation--Alaska--Juvenile literature. 3. Natural gas--Economic aspects--Alaska--Juvenile literature. I. Kiesbye, Stefan.
    HD9581.U53A454 2010
    388.5'609798--dc22
                                                                    2010003356

Printed in the United States of America
1 2 3 4 5 6 7 14 13 12 11 10

Contents

Introduction

In October 2008, a handwritten letter was sent to a newspaper office in Dawson Creek, Canada. According to the October 15, 2008, issue of *CBC News*, the anonymous writer gave EnCana Corporation and other energy companies a deadline for terminating their operations—October 11, 2008—and explained, "We will not negotiate with terrorists, which you are, as you keep endangering our families with crazy expansion of deadly gas wells in our homelands."

After the deadline expired, an explosion near EnCana's gas pipeline tore a large crater into the ground but failed to rupture the pipeline itself. Had the detonation succeeded in damaging the line, sour gas—a form of natural gas that still needs treatment to remove the toxic substance hydrogen sulfide—could have caused serious harm to the environment.

Threats to pipelines occur in all parts of the world. In August 2008, the Kurdistan Workers Party attacked the Baku-Tbilisi-Ceyhan pipeline in northern Turkey, disrupting the oil flow. On October 14, 2009, *ABC News*'s John McWethy reported that "according to U.S. and Saudi intelligence sources, a terror attack was planned on an oil pipeline that feeds Saudi Arabia's Ras Tanura terminal, the biggest oil-loading point in the world's biggest oil exporter."

Pipelines are difficult to build—they often lead through inhospitable and remote territory, sometimes cross national borders, and need to withstand extreme temperatures, earthquakes, and corrosion. As hard as it is to construct pipelines, however, it is an even more daunting task to monitor, maintain, and secure them. Leaks, which can be tough to spot, take weeks or months to repair. Also, pipelines are easy targets for criminals, who can approach them with relative ease and escape before an explosion is detected.

A case in point: The October 2008 bombing of the En-Cana gas pipeline was the sixth such occurrence, and could have proved fatal to workers trying to repair damage to the pipeline caused by an earlier blast in July of that year. David Harris, a former member of the Canadian Security Intelligence Service, told *CBC News* that the detonation pointed to a terrorist attack. "Terrorism is associated with an attempt by threat or actual violence . . . to change policy," he was quoted as saying. In his opinion, this was what happened near the British Columbia-Alberta border that weekend.

In the United States, three men were arrested for plotting an attack on Kennedy Airport in New York in 2007. According to the June 2, 2007, *New York Daily News*, the men "were targeting a massive jet-fuel pipeline that runs from Linden, N.J., through Staten Island, Brooklyn, [and Queens] to the airport. They hoped an assault on the so-called Buckeye pipeline—which carries 8 million gallons of jet fuel and refined petroleum into the city every day—would kill thousands by causing explosions through residential sections of Queens." In the aftermath of the arrests, it was debated whether the men had the means to put their plan into action, yet the plot demonstrated how vulnerable the country's gas pipelines are.

The 2008 U.S. presidential election focused heavily on America's dependency upon foreign oil, and it put the spotlight on possible alternative fuels. Although the scientific community agrees that natural gas is not a long-term solution to the country's energy demands, it is nevertheless seen as an attractive means to bridge the gap until renewable energy sources can be sufficiently developed. Many see the proposed Alaska gas pipeline, which would deliver gas from Alaska's North Slope region to the contiguous United States, as part of this solution. The viewpoints in *At Issue: The Alaska Gas Pipeline* explore issues such as safety, security, economics, and the environment as they relate to this endeavor.

1

The Future of Alaska's Gas Pipeline Is Uncertain

Elizabeth Bluemink

Elizabeth Bluemink moved to Alaska in 2004. She writes about mining, Native corporations, tourism, and other industries for the Anchorage Daily News.

The Alaska gas pipeline faces many economic and technological obstacles, but new gas reserves found throughout the American mainland could derail plans for bringing North Slope gas to the rest of the country. While many skeptics doubt the economic viability of the proposed pipeline, the developers maintain that there will be a rising demand for natural gas.

If there weren't already enough barriers to building a gas pipeline from Alaska's North Slope, the Lower 48 [contiguous United States] recently entered its biggest-ever natural gas boom.

Just as the prospects for the Alaska gas line seem to be growing brighter, new drilling techniques have unlocked vast pools of natural gas all over the Lower 48, from Texas to Pennsylvania. For now, demand isn't keeping up. Prices have swooned [dropped], and drill rigs are idling.

Pundits, politicians and industry executives have been speculating for months about what bountiful, cheap gas in the Lower 48 means for the North Slope's gas.

Emphasis on the word "speculating."

Analyzing the economic prospects of North Slope gas requires looking into a murky future that begins in 2018—the earliest year that an Alaska pipeline would be finished and North Slope gas could arrive in the market—and projecting out 30 years beyond that.

"Anything could happen between now and then," said Gary Long, a petroleum engineer who analyzes gas reserves for the U.S. Energy Information Administration.

Skeptics—including those who'd compete against Alaska's project—have raised doubts about the multibillion-dollar project. Among them is T. Boone Pickens, the legendary Texas oilman, who recently said he thinks Alaska's gas line will be delayed 10 to 15 years because of giant shale gas deposits now being exploited in Texas.

Pickens isn't exactly neutral: He's invested in the Texas gas.

The three major energy companies who hold leases to trillions of cubic feet of North Slope gas take a more optimistic view. Current conditions in the U.S. gas market aren't a factor in their decision-making, they say.

Alaska Gas Is Competitive

In the future, "We believe there will be a place for Alaska's gas," said David McDowell, a spokesman for BP [British Petroleum] and ConocoPhillips' Denali pipeline project.

As long as the costs of the pipeline project are kept under control, Alaska gas will be competitive with gas from other sources, according to Tony Palmer, a vice president for Trans-Canada Corp., a Canadian company vying with Denali to build the gas line. TransCanada was awarded a state license to develop the pipeline and recently entered into a partnership with Exxon Mobil, the North Slope's biggest gas lease holder.

The cold reality that dashed Alaska's gas pipeline dreams for decades was the low price of natural gas in Lower 48 markets.

Price is a key determinant of whether a gas line will be profitable in the future, and it's impossible to predict accurately. The best that anyone can do is plan a project that will remain profitable within a reasonable range of prices.

In a recent press conference, Palmer of TransCanada conceded that the price of gas in the Lower 48 has declined this year, but he invoked long-term forecasts that predict the price will rise again.

The major North Slope lease holders revived their interest in a gas-line project early this decade, when gas prices rose dramatically. They funded a $100 million study in 2001 to analyze potential pipeline routes.

Later that year [2001], gas prices dropped and the companies declared the project impractical. Yet the price decline was short-lived. Lower 48 natural gas prices spiked in 2005 and again last year [2008]. Prices have sunk this year [2009] as the national recession deepened, but [they] still remained well above the historic range of the 1980s and 1990s.

Prices could drop even lower in the near future, warned Porter Bennett, of Bentek Energy, a Colorado-based energy consulting firm.

"The bottom line [right now is] that we are producing a lot more gas than we are consuming. Those trends are going to continue for several years at least," Bennett said.

But what about beyond that?

The Lure of Gas

Federal forecasters and industry experts say natural gas prices will rise again, not just as a consequence of the easing of the global recession, but also due to new trends in U.S. energy consumption and a shift to costlier production methods.

Right now, some politicians and energy companies view natural gas as an attractive, cleaner alternative to two fuel sources in heavy use in the Lower 48 now—crude oil and coal—which generate a larger amount of greenhouse gas emissions, linked to global warming.

The U.S. Energy Information Administration is projecting a [2.5-trillion-cubic-foot] rise in annual demand for natural gas from 2009 to 2030. That leaves room for the roughly 1.6 trillion cubic feet a year an Alaska pipeline could supply, despite the new discoveries and production in the Lower 48.

The potential growth areas for gas in the Lower 48 are electricity generation, transportation and factories that convert natural gas into a liquid fuel, said Bennett and other oil and gas experts.

Such growth very much factors into the justifications provided by the [Alaskan governor Sarah] Palin administration and by oil companies for the need for Alaska gas.

"We have this huge lead time in front of us. The demand is, in fact, going to be there," said Joe Balash, a Palin administration special assistant on oil and gas issues.

But Alaska gas will have to compete with other suppliers who are drilling so-called "unconventional" gas sources in the Lower 48, in shale [fine-grained, sedimentary rock] and sand formations. Another potential competitor is liquified natural gas imports. The cost structure of developing and producing those two resources is different [from that of] a conventional gas project, but in the long term, the costs end up being comparable, the experts say.

Many factors still could derail Alaska's gas project or make it unprofitable.

For example, while shale gas is cheaper to develop in the short term, the costs to produce it increase over time. Drillers have to constantly poke deep holes in the ground to keep wells in production.

In the long run, the cost of developing Alaska's gas is comparable to the cost of developing shale gas or importing liquified gas, said David Hobbs, head of research for Cambridge Energy Research Associates, a global consulting firm that has advised both Exxon and the Alaska Legislature on energy issues in the past.

Also, Hobbs said, the energy giants are better positioned to tackle the expense of building [an] Alaska gas line than they were eight years ago. Thanks to high oil prices, they have much stronger balance sheets, plus Congress gave them federal loan guarantees for the project. [Hobbs] said he wouldn't argue [with the claim] that Palin administration legislation has also "been a factor in sharpening focus on the gas line issue."

Gas Everywhere

Many factors still could derail Alaska's gas project or make it unprofitable.

Chronic low gas prices. Political infighting. Construction costs that spiral out of control. North Slope lease holders refusing to commit their gas to a pipeline because it seems too risky.

TransCanada's Palmer said at a recent press conference that the builder of a pipeline has to keep the cost of gas production as low as possible and maintain a tight construction schedule, rather than waste time worrying about things it can't control.

"We think that Alaska gas can be very competitive if we can keep the (cost) of the gas down," he said.

One Alaska petroleum geologist said he's less worried about competition from shale gas than he was a few months ago.

The geologist, Dan Seamount of the Alaska Oil and Gas Conservation Commission, said he recently toured some massive natural gas fields in British Columbia with much bigger reserves than the North Slope has been calculated to hold.

"My first reaction was, 'You guys have just killed the Alaska pipeline,'" Seamount said.

But he said in recent weeks [that] he's looked at the issue a little deeper, realizing, for example, that shale gas projects in the Lower 48 face some hurdles that won't exist for a North Slope gas project. For example, activists in many Lower 48 communities have claimed that shale gas projects have contaminated their water supplies. Some Democrats in Congress this year [2009] have filed legislation to force shale gas projects to comply with stricter environmental rules.

Increasing Gas Production

No matter how much shale gas is considered recoverable, people who think it's as "easy as turning open a valve" are being overly optimistic, Seamount said. That being said, U.S. natural gas production rose by nearly 8 percent last year—its biggest increase on record, according to a recent BP report on global energy.

Last month [June 2009], a national committee of gas experts estimated that the country has a total gas resource base of 1.8 quadrillion cubic feet of known or probable gas resources—a roughly 75-year supply if consumption doesn't grow. Alaska's portion of that is about 157 trillion cubic feet of gas—a mere 11 percent, according to numbers provided [by] the group, called the Potential Gas Committee.

"We've only begun to scratch the surface of this resource," said Mark Finley, general manager of global energy markets for BP America, during a visit to Anchorage last month [June 2009].

He said it is hard to tell now how Alaska's gas line will stack up against other projects throughout the country, but he noted that natural gas has a bright future as the cleanest-burning of all fossil fuels.

"There's demand potential for sure," Finley said.

2

Alaska May Need a Natural Gas Pipeline to Avoid a Heating Disaster

Eric Lidji

Eric Lidji has reported on Alaska energy issues for the Fairbanks Daily News-Miner *and* Petroleum News. *He now lives in Pittsburgh, Pennsylvania.*

In severe weather conditions, Alaska's gas supply and distribution systems are at risk of failing. To prevent a possible disaster, several new gas pipelines have been proposed. Although many favor a gas pipeline leading through Canada to the contiguous United States, a shorter—and therefore cheaper—pipeline might help Alaskan cities meet their demand for gas in the near future. Delivering gas to mainland America might be more profitable, but volatile gas prices cast doubts on this project's long-term viability. Alaska's government must decide whether to opt for energizing the economy or for supplying its citizens with safe gas.

Just to get your attention, here's the worst-case scenario: A mid-winter cold snap hits Southcentral Alaska, bringing temperatures of 20 below zero. People from the Matanuska Valley to the Kenai Peninsula turn up their heat in unison, sucking natural gas from the Enstar Natural Gas Co. distribution grid buried beneath the city streets. This network is fed by transmission lines leading back to wells that pump natural gas from underground reservoirs across Cook Inlet. As more

Eric Lidji, "Alaska's Natural Gas Dilemma—Everyone Agrees Cook Inlet Needs Help. No One Agrees on How or Where to Get it," *Anchorage Press*, June 4, 2009. Copyright © 2009 Anchorage Press. Reproduced by permission.

people turn up the heat, engineers search for additional molecules of natural gas to manage the increased demand. But the cold doesn't let up. Then, a compressor trips at one of the major gas fields, and the pressure in the pipeline system drops below the threshold needed for making electricity. So the lights go out. System operators worry the drop in pressure allowed air to get into the grid, and federal regulations require them to stop delivering to customers. So the heat goes off.

A Bleak Scenario

The bigger problem comes next, though. To revive the system, hundreds of technicians need to go door to door to bring every customer back online one at a time, on top of a long list of other regulatory and technical requirements. It could take weeks or even months, during which time the region would be without heat or power. In winter. In Alaska. Even worse, the underground reservoirs of natural gas could be damaged from disuse, meaning [that] once the system is restored, it might never be the same again. For all the issues Alaskans worry about, none threatens as many people with consequences as extreme as this scenario. If it comes to pass, half the population of Alaska would lose heat, and even more would lose power. Industry would be crippled. It's been described as the economic equivalent of the 1964 Good Friday Earthquake.

Like every worst-case scenario, this one requires a lot of things to go wrong all at once. It's unlikely, but it's not impossible. And the chances of it happening increase every year because of the changing nature of natural gas reservoirs in the Cook Inlet basin. In fact, it's come close to happening a few times over the past decade. It came close to happening earlier this year [2009].

On January 3 [2009], temperatures dropped to 15 below across Southcentral, and the local system pulled harder on the wells and pipelines than ever before. And a compressor did fail, momentarily. In the end, the system prevailed because some things went right and some other things didn't go wrong, but industry watchers suggest we came within a few hours of a total failure.

Cook Inlet just doesn't deliver [natural gas] like it used to.

The key to understanding what almost happened is something known in industry jargon as "deliverability"—the measure of how much natural gas can be called upon at any given moment. Having large volumes of natural gas available is important because Southcentral is so dependent on it. Enstar supplies it to almost 350,000 customers. Chugach Electric Association makes 93 percent of its electricity from it. It's pulled from underground fields across the Cook Inlet and sent through transmission pipelines to the local Enstar distribution grid, where it fuels furnaces and stoves. It also travels to plants owned by Chugach and Municipal Light & Power [ML&P], who use it to run giant turbines that produce electricity for all of Anchorage. Chugach, in turns, sells electricity to smaller utilities in Homer, Seward and the Matanuska Valley, and also sends some power north to Fairbanks.

"Deliverability" Is Key to Challenges

Deliverability doesn't measure the amount of gas still underground, waiting to be brought to the surface. [That constitutes] "reserves." According to the state, Cook Inlet produced around 10.1 trillion cubic feet of gas between 1958 and 2006 and still had around 1.7 trillion cubic feet in remaining reserves as of 2007, the most recent figures available. Think of reserves as a giant tank of water, and of deliverability as a fire hose. If the stream [from] the hose is weak, it doesn't matter how much water is in the tank: The house will burn down.

The Cook Inlet natural gas system is like a living organism connecting your furnace to underground reservoirs. Producers like Marathon, Chevron and ConocoPhillips constantly monitor wells, gauging the amount of gas remaining in each reservoir and the amount of pressure available to help bring that natural gas up to the surface. Buyers like Enstar and Chugach do similar monitoring on their pipelines and power plants. These figures all change constantly. Reservoirs lose pressure as they age, like a deflating balloon, making each new molecule harder to retrieve. The biggest gas fields in the Cook Inlet are more than 40 years old. Cook Inlet just doesn't deliver like it used to.

The problem isn't a lack of solutions. It's an abundance of them.

January's [2009] cold snap highlighted the problem. With temperatures averaging 11 below zero, the Cook Inlet basin delivered around 440 million cubic feet of natural gas. On February 3, 1999, a day with even colder temperatures, the basin delivered 763 million cubic feet of natural gas. That's a 42 percent decline over the course of a decade. And the pace is increasing. Over the past two years, deliverability has declined around 21 percent.

The problem of declining deliverability is widely acknowledged by the industry. Enstar, the electric companies and the gas producers all talk about it publicly. At an industry conference in Anchorage last November [2008], Steve Wright, the manager of Chevron's assets in Alaska, said that the four largest Cook Inlet gas fields delivered around 14 billion cubic feet in January 2004, but less than 9 billion cubic feet in September 2008. Wright said Cook Inlet deliverability is falling at a rate of 8 to 14 percent, depending on how you slice it, a trend line he said is "quite alarming for all residents in the Anchorage bowl."

Tony Izzo, the former head of Enstar and now a local consultant, explained it this way to the Anchorage Assembly last November [2008]: "We're only as strong as the weakest link in the energy infrastructure, and the weakest link right now is deliverability."

The problem isn't a lack of solutions. It's an abundance of them.

Debating the Solutions

The debate going on right now among producers, utilities, regulators and the government is about the best way to solve this problem, knowing on the one hand that time is of the essence and on the other hand that Alaska will be stuck with its decision for decades. The solutions fall into two general categories: bolstering Cook Inlet or supplementing it.

Bolstering Cook Inlet means getting the basin to do more. One way is by artificially increasing the pressure of the natural gas using compressors, allowing a smaller amount of gas to flow with the ease of larger quantities. But while these compressors alleviate the problem, they don't solve it entirely. On occasion, a compressor can fail suddenly, or "trip," for several hours, causing drops in pressure. A compressor at the Beluga River field, one of the largest and oldest in the region, has tripped at least 12 times since being installed in April 2007, according to two area companies that depend on the unit.

Another way to improve deliverability is to decrease the need for natural gas by making power plants that run better, retrofitting buildings to be more efficient and training customers to conserve. "This isn't always about the supply side. It's the demand side also," Carri Lockhart, Alaska production manager for Marathon, said in late March [2009].

Another way to improve deliverability is to have gas available any time. This means increasing storage. One of the primary challenges for heating Alaska is managing the extreme swings between summer and winter demand. Storage facilities allow producers to pull natural gas from the ground at a more measured pace from month to month, limiting stress on the reservoirs. Enstar could then use extra gas produced during the summer to meet increased demand in the winter. Storage facilities are expensive, though. Enstar estimates that the investments needed to offset declines in gas supplies anticipated in 2011 would cost somewhere in the neighborhood of $25 million to $100 million.

In addition to a few traditional storage facilities across the Cook Inlet, there is also a major makeshift storage unit already in operation. It's a 42-year-old facility in Nikiski that super-chills natural gas into a liquid state and loads it onto barges that sail across the Pacific Ocean to feed power companies in Tokyo. This facility, owned jointly by ConocoPhillips and Marathon, frustrates some state lawmakers, who cannot reconcile shipping natural gas to Asia while business leaders complain about declining supplies and looming shortfalls in Alaska. In early May [2009], three Anchorage-area Democratic senators—Bill Wielechowski, Johnny Ellis and Bettye Davis— asked the [Alaska Governor Sarah] Palin administration to require Cook Inlet producers to sell gas to Alaska utilities before shipping it to Asia.

But the senators also acknowledged one of the key benefits of the plant: It's viewed by many as being the last line of defense against system failure. During cold snaps, natural gas is diverted from the plant into the local grid. These diversions have kept the system afloat several times over the past decade, but like the rest of the system, the plant has less natural gas flowing through it each year. During the 1999 cold snap, the plant held 224 million cubic feet of natural gas. During the cold snap this year [2009], it held only 40 million cubic feet.

Drilling New Wells

This plant is the only export facility of its kind in the country, and every so often the owners of it must return to the federal government to get renewed permission to ship domestic gas overseas. This export license was set to expire this year [2009], but the companies got it extended to 2011 with the backing of the Palin administration. In return for its support, the administration told ConocoPhillips and Marathon to drill new wells in aging fields. The goal was to increase deliverability, just as two straws suck faster than one straw. The companies followed through, but haven't released the results yet. And Marathon has already said it plans to drill half as many wells this year as last year.

As the big players expand old fields, several smaller companies believe there are still undiscovered reservoirs in Cook Inlet. But companies . . . large and small say they have little incentive to drill in Cook Inlet because they can't get a competitive price for gas.

Which gets to the heart of a decades-long debate: What is Cook Inlet gas really worth?

The hearing room of the Legislative Information Office in Anchorage was nearly packed on the afternoon of November 25, 2008, two days before Thanksgiving. Small business owners filled the front rows, followed by regulators and public advocates, and executives from Enstar, Chugach, ConocoPhillips and Marathon. It was a hearing before the Senate Judiciary Committee called by its chair, Senator Hollis French. French had recently received an email from Adam Galindo, vice president of Taco Loco in Anchorage. French paraphrased the message: "They're saying I'm not going to have gas in a month. I make tacos for a living. How am I supposed to figure out where to get a gas supply?"

Local gas supplier Aurora Power Resources had announced plans to drop around 400 commercial customers, effective December 1 [2008]. Enstar offered to supply those customers, but only through the end of the year. Enstar couldn't legally offer service in 2009, it said, because regulations prohibited the company from adding customers if it didn't already have gas under contract to meet the additional demand. Enstar said it didn't have the gas.

The business owners understood they were collateral damage in a larger battle. "There's an old saying in Africa about how when elephants fight only the grass gets tromped, and that's kind of where I feel I am today," said Mike Gordon, owner of the bar Chilkoot Charlie's. Enstar agreed, but said the fight was bigger and longer than most people realized. "We feel like we are the grass underneath the elephants, also," Dan Dieckgraeff, the manager of rates and regulatory affairs for Enstar, said during testimony.

The prolific gas fields in the Cook Inlet were found by accident in the 1950s and 1960s, the consequence of early oil exploration.

Enstar had been trying to get more gas supplies for years. In fact, for the six months prior to the November [2008] hearing, Enstar had been knee-deep in filings to convince state regulators to let it buy gas from Marathon and ConocoPhillips. And just a few weeks before the hearing, on Halloween, the regulators agreed, but only on the condition that Enstar negotiate a different price for the gas. The regulators told Enstar to make the changes to the contracts by December 1 [2008].

Alaska Is an Exceptional Region

This scene would be unlikely anywhere in the United States except Alaska, because the natural gas market in Cook Inlet is fundamentally different than [in] the rest of the country. The Lower 48 gas market is highly liquid, meaning there are many buyers looking for the best deal and many sellers competing against each other to offer the best deal. As a result, prices constantly change as buyers leave one supplier for another, as sellers try to out-price their competitors, as explorers find new reservoirs and as pipeline builders make more efficient connections. The price at any given time is called the spot market.

There has never been a spot market for natural gas in Alaska. The prolific gas fields in the Cook Inlet were found by accident in the 1950s and 1960s, the consequence of early oil exploration. Unable to sell this gas on the world market, companies signed long contracts with Anchorage-area utilities, supplying the region with relatively cheap natural gas at a stable price. Over the decades since, though, these original contracts expired and, after negotiations, were replaced with new, usually more expensive contracts, leading to steadily increasing gas and electricity bills throughout the region (although still typically below Lower 48 prices). (ML&P charges less for electricity than Chugach because ML&P bought a share of the Beluga gas field in the 1990s.) These overlapping and leap-frogging contracts means there is no spot market for natural gas in Alaska. Instead, producers and local utilities negotiate supply contracts, which state regulators either approve or reject. . . .

The RCA [Regulatory Commission of Alaska] is looking at ways to resolve the pricing problem, including the possibility of creating a standard contract to alleviate the uncertainty facing producers and utilities. Everyone agrees pricing must be reconciled, regardless of the future of Cook Inlet. Declining deliverability can be fixed by replacing Cook Inlet gas with North Slope gas, but new gas still needs a price and there still won't be a spot market. Even fuel from proposed renewable energy projects—like wind and geothermal—will need a price.

With all those headaches, it makes sense that Enstar is interested in looking beyond Cook Inlet for natural gas. Without new supply contracts, Enstar faces a shortfall in 2011. Even with new contracts, Enstar is projecting regional demand will outpace Cook Inlet supplies by 2015. This is the argument for supplementing Cook Inlet, rather than just bolstering it.

It's long been assumed the North Slope would eventually provide relief to Southcentral in the form of a major gas pipeline running from Prudhoe Bay to Outside [non-Alaska] markets. Along the route of this big pipeline, take-off points would allow Alaska communities to tap the pipeline for local use. In March 2008, though, Enstar signaled its impatience with this game plan, saying it was looking into building a "smaller" pipeline to bring a northern natural gas supply directly into Anchorage, without worrying about hitching local needs onto a project bound for Outside markets. This project is now called the "bullet line."

"We need gas sooner rather than later," Colleen Starring, Enstar's regional vice president, told an industry group in May 2008. "If there were another discovery in the Inlet that's great, but we can't wait for that to happen."

Every pipeline needs a supply. Enstar is focused on the Gubik Complex, a series of natural gas fields dotting the northern foothills of the Brooks Range. Government drilling crews discovered Gubik in the early 1950s, and entrepreneurs in Fairbanks at the time looked at developing the field, but decided the numbers didn't pan out. Anadarko Petroleum Co., a large exploration company out of Houston, arrived in the area in 1998, picking up more than 3 million acres in leases. The company drilled its first Gubik wells in early 2008 and returned to drill more wells this year [2009]. The program is unprecedented. All previous gas discoveries in northern Alaska have been accidents, or byproducts of the search for oil. Never before has a company specifically targeted gas in northern Alaska.

The reason for that is simple: there is no way to sell natural gas from northern Alaska, because there is no way to get that natural gas to market. For that reason, many saw

Anadarko's decision to spend tens of millions of dollars looking for gas it can't currently sell as the company showing faith in various efforts to build a big pipeline, including the Alaska Gasline Inducement Act, or AGIA, Governor Sarah Palin's 2007 effort to move the project along. Since Anadarko began exploring the region, two competing projects have emerged, the TransCanada effort under AGIA and the Denali project outside of AGIA.

The Bullet Line Project

Enstar's bullet line intrigues Anadarko. It gives the company an alternative if the big pipeline fails or gets delayed. Also, the bullet line offers a financial incentive. Cook Inlet producers currently get a tax break for gas they sell within Alaska. In November 2007, state lawmakers extended that break to the rest of the state, meaning Anadarko would pay lower taxes if it ships its gas through a bullet line, rather than through a big pipeline.

Just like you pay a toll to drive on certain roads, producers pay a toll to ship their gas through a pipeline.

While Enstar looks at this direct bullet line from northern Alaska, other groups continue to pursue the original plan for Anchorage: a spur coming off the proposed big pipeline.

A spur line has an advantage over a bullet line: it's cheaper. It's cheaper for several reasons. First, it's shorter. A bullet line would need to be 800 miles or longer to stretch from northern fields to Anchorage, while a spur would be around 460 miles long.

Second, the spur line is cheaper because it takes advantage of economies of scale on the big pipeline. Market prices . . . only represent the cost of the actual commodity of gas, not the additional cost to move it from fields to homes. Just like you pay a toll to drive on certain roads, producers pay a toll to ship their gas through a pipeline. These tolls, known in the pipeline world as tariffs, let a company like Enstar recover the cost of building a pipeline and also earn a profit. Producers pay these tariffs, but ultimately pass the cost on to you.

So a cheaper pipeline means cheaper gas for consumers. But so does a busier pipeline. As more customers buy gas, the fixed costs of the pipeline get spread over more people. If two pipelines cost the same amount to build, but one carries more gas than the other, that gas would be cheaper to buy. Volume tempers the cost . . . .

Questions Surface About the Government's Plans

Upon taking office in late 2006, the Palin administration said the big pipeline would address the needs of Alaska consumers. Earlier this year, though, the administration took a more active role in efforts to build an in-state pipeline, hiring someone to coordinate the various efforts of ANGDA [Alaska Natural Gas Development Authority] and Enstar. The administration says it still expects AGIA to deliver a pipeline, it just doesn't know if the pipeline will come soon enough to address shortfalls. This raises questions: Why anchor Alaska to a costly bullet line if the administration believes the cheaper option will eventually materialize? Why not look instead for a bridge between now and the time a big pipeline starts shipping gas? Enstar is looking into importing gas for a few years starting in 2011. Why not import for a few more? Wouldn't consumers be willing to pay higher prices for a few years if it meant lower prices for decades to come?

The administration believes it is being prudent. "If we don't start working on it now, it may be too late to consider that as an option in 2011 or 2012 when we know what our choices really are," Joe Balash, Palin's assistant for oil and gas issues, told lawmakers in April [2009].

Speaking to reporters on the last day of the session, Palin framed the issue differently: "Alaskans may at some point be asked to make a choice here: Do we want to import natural gas for use to energize our economy, our homes, our businesses? Or do we want to commercialize our own Alaskan-owned natural gas?" In a recent op-ed in the *Anchorage Daily News*, Palin said she wasn't "walking away" from anything, not the big pipeline, not the spur line and not efforts to ship liquefied natural gas from Valdez, the "all-Alaska line." Palin wrote, "We are reviewing all options to ensure Alaskans know all the facts about progress to flow gas to our homes and businesses." The basic dilemma is the wallet versus the watch. A spur line promises cheaper gas but is dependent on a large, expensive, complicated project. A bullet line is independent, but its independence will likely make it more expensive. And while imports can be temporary, these pipeline projects are permanent. They're almost certainly mutually exclusive, as well; Alaska will be stuck with whichever one ultimately gets built.

In the meantime, it's summer in Anchorage again. Long hours of sunlight mean less electricity, and rising mercury means lower natural gas bills. It's a temporary reprieve, of course. Come October, winter will creep back over the city, and when it does, Southcentral Alaska either will—or won't—be ready for another big cold snap.

3

Without Fiscal Certainty, Alaska Will Lose Out on Its Pipeline

Andrew Halcro

Andrew Halcro served in the Alaska House of Representatives from 1999 to 2003, and he ran for governor in 2006 as an independent.

A gas pipeline has been an Alaskan priority since the introduction of the Alaska Gasline Inducement Act, the state's initiative to expedite development of Alaska's gas resources. Yet by offering guaranteed tax incentives for only ten years, the government might discourage developers from building the pipeline. Fiscal certainty is important to companies producing gas and ones building the pipeline, and Alaska has to act fast if it wants to avoid failure. Lawmakers need to have the authority to grant more favorable terms to developers.

This week [June 2009] Alaska lawmakers took testimony about the progress of Alaska's Natural Gas Pipeline from the [Governor Sarah] Palin administration as well as [from] the oil and gas companies that hold the leases to develop the North Slope's gas reserves.

As they have since the introduction of the Alaska Gasline Inducement Act (AGIA) [an initiative to expedite the development of Alaska's gas resources], the Palin administration testified that they view the economics of the pipeline project as profitable, and the state didn't need to make any concessions to attract investment.

Meanwhile, as they have since the introduction of AGIA, oil and gas companies reiterated their need for fiscal certainty before committing to pay for the largest and most expensive energy project in the world.

But with the Palin administration locked into AGIA, [Alaska] Revenue Commissioner Pat Galvin told lawmakers that those who will accept the risk don't need any more certainty other than what currently exists because the state's economic analysis shows the project is deep in the money.

This disagreement demands a closer look.

"Fuzzy Math"

The state's economic modeling that Galvin is touting has always been viewed by some as fuzzy math. During testimony last summer [2008], producers offered a number of areas where the state's analysis failed to account for risk.

It's not just oil and gas companies [that] are pointing out flaws in the state's economic modeling.

On July 11, 2008, Exxon's Marty Massey testified the state's economic analysis was based on "simplifying assumptions." The analysis ignores the reality of the real risk that firm transportation commitments represent, by classifying them as normal operating expenses. Massey stated that under the proper analysis, the net present value to his company isn't $13.5 billion as stated in the state's analysis, but zero.

State Senator Gene Terriault asked Massey if it was true that those FT's [firm transportation commitments] represented just a footnote on their balance sheet. Yes Massey replied, but the entire footnote currently existing on Exxon's balance sheet today is $3 billion. With this project it would increase to almost $80 billion, which makes a dramatic difference.

John Zager, of Chevron, put the risk in perspective. The reliance on net present value as the state has done is only one way companies look at the economics of the project. Firm transportation commitments represent a real transfer of value that in this case would equal upwards of $125 billion. This is quickly approaching the market cap of both Chevron and Conoco, Zager stated.

And it's not just oil and gas companies [that] are pointing out flaws in the state's economic modeling.

The State's Economic Viability Exaggerated

In a paper to be published in the September 2009 edition of the *Journal of Economic Issues*, Roger Marks, a former Department of Revenue petroleum economist, will lay out the case of how the administration's analysis "overstated the economic vitality of the project and hence understated the severity of the commercial issues."

Second, Galvin's defense of maintaining the status quo with regard to tax rates and certainty seem at odds with prior testimony and reality.

During testimony on AGIA in April of 2007, Department of Revenue Commissioner Pat Galvin was asked about the state's existing gas-tax rate. Galvin replied, "Our level of confidence in the current tax rate is relatively low."

A few days later in the House Resources Committee, lawmakers queried Galvin about why the state wouldn't make necessary adjustments to the tax rate before asking for competitive bids under AGIA.

With all the concerns about the lack of fiscal predictability in AGIA, why wouldn't you want to nail down something as critical as tax rates, asked one Representative. How do you expect someone to submit a complete bid if they don't know what their tax rates are going to be, asked another.

"You have moved from a question of whether the producers need to have this level of certainty that they keep talking about at the time they submit the application or whether it's at the time they commit their gas. What we have structured in the bill is that level of certainty we believe is appropriate at the time they commit their gas," Galvin answered.

Disagreement over Tax Rates

Twenty-four hours after Galvin said the state had determined that it wasn't important for AGIA applicants to know the actual tax rate, the House Resources Committee took testimony from a prospective applicant who disagreed and told the committee just how critical it is for private companies in the real world.

"To make a sound and fundamentally good decision, I have to know," replied Marty Massey from Exxon when asked about the importance of knowing the tax rate. "I don't know, I really don't know what rate to run the economics at because it can change, all of it can change."

Nine months later, on January 19, 2008, Marcia Davis, Deputy Revenue Commissioner, testified in front of the Senate Resources Committee. Davis was asked if the legislature should begin discussions about changing the gas tax in anticipation of open season. "Beginning the gas-talk discussion is certainly not inappropriate," she said. Davis went on to admit that the tax rate "affects what a producer puts into their consideration as they approach an open season and decide whether to tender their gas."

Isn't that exactly what Marty Massey from Exxon said almost a year earlier when the producers were advocating changes to AGIA to make it commercially viable so they could offer a competitive bid? Yes, it was.

However, the administration's strategy has been to try and force the producers to accept the terms of AGIA by committing their gas to a TransCanada pipeline in exchange for a favorable tax structure.

The problem for the administration is that its bluff is transparent.

"The horse is already out of the barn, we've already picked someone with whom we've partnered," said Kurt Gibson, deputy director of the Alaska Division of Oil and Gas, in an August 8, 2008, interview with CNN. "The TransCanada pipeline is the vehicle for fiscal certainty."

A Political Bluff

The problem for the administration is that its bluff is transparent. Legally, the state can't adopt a tax structure that applies only to those who agree to commit their gas to TransCanada's pipeline. That would violate just about every equal access provision and restraint of trade clause. Once the legislature adopts a tax structure, it will apply to all of the producers regardless of AGIA.

For the administration, the gas tax rate and corresponding fiscal certainty is viewed as a tool to be used to leverage the producers to commit gas to a TransCanada pipeline, thus forcing a marriage governed by the uneconomical vows of AGIA. As Roger Marks will highlight in his soon-to-be released economic analysis of AGIA, "you cannot make a bad project good by borrowing money."

Last year [2008] during legislative hearings on AGIA, questions about adopting new gas tax rates or fiddling around with fiscal certainty drew an animated response from Commissioner Galvin. "Don't do it," Galvin warned during committee testimony last June. "Don't think you're going to get cute and walk right up to that line, because we will have to pay TransCanada treble damages," he added.

Alaska lawmakers must exercise their authority as a separate branch of government and begin evaluating the tax certainty question on their own, without the administration.

Being handcuffed by the terms of AGIA will continue to be the way not to get a natural gas pipeline project built. The attempt to force-feed the producers TransCanada and their AGIA mandates will continue to risk delays in getting to the all-important final investment decision.

It's evidenced in that this week [June 2009] Alaska lawmakers heard the same comments from stakeholders regarding fiscal terms as they heard two years ago before they voted to pass AGIA. Even with all the pomp and circumstance surrounding Exxon's announced partnership with TransCanada two weeks ago the only thing that has changed since the introduction of AGIA is the date on the calendar.

Necessary Steps to Solve the Problem

Alaska lawmakers must exercise their authority as a separate branch of government and begin evaluating the tax certainty question on their own, without the administration. Failing to do so allows the administration to continuing leading Alaska's gas pipeline hopes down the primrose path [to deceive, lead astray].

State Senator Bert Stedman (R-Sitka) just recently returned from a five-day seminar on World Fiscal Systems for Oil & Gas, which focused on quantitative analysis and a critical review of oil- and gas-producing regions throughout the world. Stedman, who will play a key role in determining state gas tax policy, shouldn't wait to begin substantive legislative conversations apart from the administration to begin the inevitable task of addressing the state's gas-tax structure.

And for those who doubt the need for lawmakers to engage, consider where we are after three years.

Since 2006, Governor Sarah Palin and others like DNR [Department of Natural Resources] Commissioner Tom Irwin have been critical of former Governor Frank Murkowski's proposed gas-line deal, which included offering the producers 35 years of fiscal certainty. Critics claimed extended fiscal certainty gave away state sovereignty and thus was the primary reason . . . AGIA was created.

So after years of promoting AGIA as the only way to get around having to offer Murkowski-esque terms in order to secure commitments from oil and gas companies to build the Alaska Natural Gas Pipeline, has the gas-line paradigm been changed by AGIA?

In addressing the length of fiscal certainty needed to secure commitments from oil and gas companies, Exxon's Marty Massey told lawmakers this week [June 2009], "Thirty-five years will be acceptable, 10 years not." BP's Claire Fitzpatrick stated that they would want the length of certainty to reflect the length of their financial commitments.

Fiscal Certainty

The answer is that AGIA hasn't changed the paradigm at all. The producers' permanent interests have remained just that— permanent.

Since gas-line discussion began under the Palin administration, producers have consistently testified that 10 years was not enough time to guarantee a tax regime for the most expensive oil and gas project in the world.

After all, if 10 years is enough certainty for the producers as far as the Palin administration is concerned, why is Trans-Canada requiring 25 years of certainty from the producers?

Since TransCanada, according to AGIA, is requiring 25-year financial commitments from gas shippers to build the pipeline, it stands to reason that gas shippers would require a commensurate commitment, [as] they are the ones paying for the construction and assuming the risk.

The prevailing legal theory is that the legislature may be able to approve locking in tax rates up to 10 years without stirring up constitutional concerns and a possible rebuke from the Alaska State Supreme Court. While initially AGIA granted gas shippers a 10-year fix on tax terms, the legislature removed the provision from the bill before passage, so today there is no enforceable guarantee. The State Senate's removal of the 10-year guarantee was due to questions about whether lawmakers could even approve a 10-year tax freeze without exposing themselves to a constitutional challenge.

With that in mind, the legislature should consider putting [before voters] a constitutional amendment ... in the 2010 election that allows for a very narrow exception to allow lawmakers to grant longer tax certainty in order to facilitate the gas pipeline construction in the case lawmakers decide it is ultimately necessary.

The amendment, if approved, would appear on the November 2010 ballot and, if passed by voters, would enable lawmakers more authority to offer terms that are more conducive to the risk associated with the magnitude of this project.

With the offer of 10 years' worth of fiscal certainty being legally questionable, as well as a non-starter with stakeholders who will assume the risk, this issue will need to be resolved sooner rather than later. Gas shippers will not commit to the project unless they have confidence that any tax regime will withstand a legal challenge.

Timing Is Important

With two open seasons scheduled for 2010 and both predicted to fail, due to a lack of agreement on fiscal terms and certainty, timing is critical.

Positive movement on granting lawmakers more legal room to move would ensure they have all the tools they may need, and thus would avoid getting pushed back for years to address what will be the pivotal sticking point in achieving Alaska's goal of a natural gas pipeline.

Alaska Needs a Gas-to-Liquid (GTL) Plant to Complement a Pipeline

Richard Peterson

Richard Peterson is the president, CEO, and managing member of Alaska Natural Resources to Liquids.

As enormous gas resources are being discovered all across mainland America, the need for a pipeline bringing Alaska gas to the contiguous United States diminishes. Yet Alaska gas could be profitably turned into synthetic transportation fuels, if the legislature gives incentives to build a world-scale gas-to-liquids (GTL) plant. Such a plant would benefit from the growing alternative transportation fuel market and make Alaska gas recession-proof.

The State of Alaska has been pushing for a gas line from the North Slope through Fairbanks to the lower 48 [contiguous United States] with a spur line to Anchorage to supply Alaskan gas to these markets. The State recently through the AGIA [Alaska Gasline Inducement Act, an initiative to expedite the development of Alaska's gas resources] process selected TransCanada to lead an effort to apply for FERC [Federal Energy Regulatory Commission] certification of this gas pipeline. Unfortunately, the economy, [gas discoveries in the lower 48] and the market are not cooperating to justify the big gas line to the lower 48. To add to Alaska's problems, gas reserves in the Cook Inlet continue to decline, with no new major gas field discoveries.

Many in Alaska think the lower 48 desperately needs Alaskan gas or will need it within 10 years. They fail to recognize that the U.S. imports very little natural gas, less than 1% of its pre-recession needs, and more importantly [that] recent advances in horizontal drilling in the enormous gas-shale [fine-grained, sedimentary rock] formations stretching from Texas to New York will add trillions of cubic feet of gas reserves to the U.S. supply picture. A June 18th [2009] natural gas reserve report by the nonprofit Potential Gas Committee indicated that the amount of natural gas available for production in the United States has soared 58% in the past four years, driven by a drilling boom and the discovery of huge new gas fields in Texas, Louisiana and Pennsylvania, a new study says.

Alaska Gas Might Be Too Expensive

Worse for Alaska North Slope gas is that much of these gas-shale reserves can be developed for less than the price needed to support the Alaska gas line and, still worse, these new gas reserves are much closer to the market. [P]lus, [they] can be developed to meet an increase in market demand on an incremental, year-by-year basis.

Because the Alaska gas line may be delayed for decades, several groups have begun looking at building a "bullet" gas line from the North Slope through Fairbanks and on to Anchorage to supply a new energy resource to Fairbanks and supplement the Cook Inlet gas reserves for Southcentral.

The bullet line estimated to cost $3 [billion] to $4 billion, will need a base load gas market approaching 500–800 million cubic feet per day to economically justify the project. Depending upon both the annual and peak gas demand for Fairbanks and the decline of the Cook Inlet gas resource, the commercial base lead market may need to cut back operations during peak cold days unless new gas reserves are made available. Couple [with that] the fact that Alaska is probably the second-most-expensive place in the U.S. to build and operate an industrial plant and, not to mention, [the nation is undergoing] possibly the worst recession America has faced in the past 70 years: it is doubtful any commercial gas user will relocate to Alaska to act as a base load market.

It seems that the market is conspiring against Alaska's dream of delivering North Slope natural gas to the lower 48 and to its citizens.

But all is not lost.

A Different Approach

Years ago [s]enators [Ted] Stevens and [Lisa] Murkowski, along with Congressman [Don] Young, introduced legislation to support the Alaska gas line and in 2005, provide economic support for the Fischer-Tropsch (F-T) process. The F-T process, developed by the Germans in the early 1920s and commercialized by South Africa in the mid-1950s can convert natural gas (coal and biomass also) into synthetic transportation fuels. Many in Alaska don't realize that almost 70% of the gasoline and diesel sold in the U.S. comes from imported crude oil. [T]herefore it can be said the U.S. desperately needs alternative transportation fuels made from domestic resources today.

Perhaps a different approach is needed to get Alaska North Slope gas (hydrocarbons) to lower 48 energy markets (in a different form, i.e. transportation fuels), while also supporting a bullet line through Fairbanks to Anchorage sooner [rather] than later.

Alaska Natural Resources to Liquids (ANRTL), a long proponent of the F-T process to develop Alaska resources and reduce U.S. dependence upon imported crude oil believes that by combining:

- The economic support put in place by the Alaska Delegation for the gas line

- The economic support put in place for F-T fuels also by the Alaska Delegation

- Lower excise taxes levied on natural gas transportation fuels

- With a proven F-T technology provider, along with

- The Alaska Railroad's bonding authority, and

- A gas pipeline company capable of developing the 800-plus-mile bullet gas line

A world-scale gas-to-liquids (GTL) plant requiring 700 million cubic feet per day could be developed that would anchor the bullet line, supply 70,000 barrels per day (more than 1 billion gallons per year) of EPA-approved non-toxic transportation fuels to Alaska and [to] lower 48 markets, plus eliminate the current price premium Alaskans pay for gasoline and diesel over lower 48 prices. By basing the "first" GTL module on proven North Slope natural gas, you will need 7.5 Tcf [trillion cubic feet] for a 30-year supply.

The market for alternative transportation fuels that will actually reduce U.S. imports of crude oil is almost unlimited, even in today's recession.

Cook Inlet natural gas producers/developers take heart; you find another 350 million per day (2.5 Tcf) of natural gas to support an expansion of the GTL facility and ANRTL will add an additional GTL module. Cook Inlet producers will see a market, a GTL plant, know it's real and spend the capital to explore for Cook Inlet gas reserves. Still other proven GTL technology could be applied to the mothballed [not in use] Agrium [major retailer of agricultural products] facility to produce value-added transportation fuels worth far more than fertilizer at much lower gas-supply levels than a GTL module would require.

Three important points Alaskans should know when discussing North Slope natural gas delivery to the lower 48:

1. GTLs will actually reduce U.S. energy imports.

Less than 1% of America's natural gas needs are imported, while almost 70% of America's transportation fuel needs are imported. Alternative transportation fuels made from Alaska North Slope natural gas will reduce U.S. energy imports on a [one-for-one] basis.

2. GTLs have a higher market value.

One million Btu's [British thermal units; a traditional measurement of energy] of natural gas in the lower 48 sells for $4.50 per unit, while diesel fuel in California currently sells for $14 per unit at the refinery outlet. Value-added processes such as a GTL program will benefit Alaskans from a jobs and value-to-the-state-treasury perspective.

3. GTLs have an unlimited market in [the United States] today, tomorrow and 20 years from now.

The market for alternative transportation fuels that will actually reduce U.S. imports of crude oil is almost unlimited, even in today's recession. If Anchorage, Fairbanks, the Alaska Delegation, North Slope gas owners, Enstar, Alaska Legislature and [the Alaska Governor Sarah] Palin Administration all act together, a gas line from the North Slope through Fairbanks to Anchorage, with a world-scale GTL plant anchor tenant, can happen today, not 5 or 10 or 15 or even 20 years from now.

5

The Alaska Gas
Pipeline Should Not Lead
Through Canada

Joseph Keefe

Joseph Keefe is the editor in chief of The Maritime Executive.

Building a gas pipeline leading from Alaska through Canada to the contiguous United States is a dangerous project. It puts a foreign country in charge of American gas delivery and makes the pipeline vulnerable to foreign terrorists. A shorter pipeline to Valdez and subsequent transportation by ship might be a better alternative. America needs to protect its interests and ensure any pipeline's safety. A pipeline between Chicago and the North Slope is not the solution.

Finally, it looks like billions of cubic feet of stranded gas may be on the way down from Alaska's North Slope. From my perspective, the best way to do that is to take it down to Valdez and send it out by ship. On the other hand, the old adage that says that no other means of moving oil in large volumes can compete with a pipeline still rings true. Nevertheless, the longer the trip and the more sources and destinations required, the smaller the chances anyone will build it. Today, there are even a couple of other variables in play, as well. Why anyone (trying to lessen our dependence on foreign oil) would also ignore either one is simply beyond comprehension.

This week's [July 2009] report that yet another attack on natural gas pipelines has occurred shouldn't necessarily surprise anyone. That these events are taking place, not in *Colombia*, but instead in the Canadian Province of *British Columbia* should. Characterized by Canadian authorities as "domestic terrorism," at least six bombings of natural gas pipelines in northeastern British Columbia in Canada have been reported since last October [2008]. A $500,000 reward in place for information leading to the prosecution of those responsible for bombings of the pipelines has yet to realize any joy, and there is little reason to think that the Royal Canadian Mounted Police (RCMP) are any closer to catching the criminals today than they were nine months ago.

The decision to move U.S. natural resources overland through a foreign country is a curious one.

Separately and back in Washington, support for a proposed $30 billion pipeline project that will take North Slope natural gas 1,700 miles through Alaska and Canada and then on down to the midwestern United States is gathering steam. [Because it is a]nything but a done deal, the task will involve market forces, state and national politics and a host of environmental and regulatory hurdles before the project can move forward. Two consortiums, each consisting of at least two oil majors, are bidding to become the primary contractor for the massive project. Long since forgotten, except for the occasional talk of a "small spurline to Valdez" is the viable option of bringing the gas to market through the established deepwater port of Valdez, [Alaska].

The decision to move U.S. natural resources overland through a foreign country is a curious one. Instead of building a far shorter (800 miles) and far less expensive pipeline alongside the existing Trans-Alaska crude pipeline (TAPS), which moves crude oil from Alaska's North Slope down to

Valdez, the powers-that-be have decided on a project that will take much longer. In Alaska, most of the necessary right-of-way hurdles have already been jumped, whereas—noting the domestic terrorism ongoing in Canada—that task is still very much a work in progress for our northern neighbor. But, there are other, more compelling reasons not to go the overland route.

Pipelines Have Severe Drawbacks

Oil pipelines also move oil safely and reliably, but not without some drawbacks. High on the list comes an almost complete lack of flexibility. For example, if market conditions change, customers disappear or the gas wells themselves play out, the fixed pipeline cannot adapt. Indeed. And unlike the Valdez option, where the infrastructure to move this gas via ship to any number of markets already exists, gas moved from the North Slope through Canada can [have only] one destination—unless, of course, the Canadians decide to build their own spurlines to existing Canadian markets.

The dangers inherent in depending on commodities shipped via pipeline overland through a foreign country are many. Just ask the EU [European Union] about their gas supplies that move westward from the old Soviet bloc [nations that once belonged to the now-disbanded Union of Soviet Socialist Republics]. It doesn't take much of a political spat to get the valve pinched in or perhaps shut altogether, usually in the dead of winter. And, while no one is suggesting that the Canadians would consider that option the next time the timber dispute comes to a head, questions of security must be answered before laying that first foot of steel cylinder across the border. Today, there are less people living in British Columbia than there are in just a couple of New York City's boroughs, and yet, after the better part of one year, the perpetrators of the violent pipeline crimes have still not been identified. Frankly, I'm more concerned about this than I am about anything else.

Well beyond the issues of national security and keeping firm control of our own natural resources [lies] the questionable wisdom of spending billions of dollars in Canada when the domestic U.S. economy remains on life support. And, shipping gas through Valdez also has the added punch of possibly reinvigorating a domestic shipbuilding boom. Sure, much of the gas would be exported on foreign bottoms [ships] only to return on cargo swaps (also on foreign-built vessels) to the United States, but if MARAD [Maritime Administration] can demand that U.S. sailors be employed on foreign flag tonnage [ships] to satisfy licensing demands for import facilities in the Lower 48 [contiguous United States], they can exert similar pressures here, as well.

It is time to shift course and protect our own interests.

The Colonial Pipeline, a 48-inch clean-products [jet fuel, gasoline, and other light, refined oil derivatives] line stretching from the Gulf Coast all the way to the U.S. East Coast, does the work of as many as 150 vessels. And that metric may well be true for an overland gas line, as well. Today, the primary mission for the Office of the U.S. Federal Coordinator is to expedite construction of the gas pipeline that will commercialize North Slope gas and bring it to the Lower 48 domestic markets. That decision has already been made. The most optimistic guess for when all of that could happen is 2018, but in reality, and given the politics of the matter, we're probably looking at five years beyond that, at the earliest.

Protecting Alaska's Interests

Perhaps the best we can hope for in terms of keeping some control over all of that "stranded" domestic gas is a smaller spurline to Valdez. If and when that happens, at least we'll have the domestic option of effecting some limited cargo swaps so as to send gas to East and Gulf coast markets when the valve closes between Chicago and the North Slope. And that day will come—assuming that they can ever get the pipeline built in the first place.

It's taken 30+ years to bully the oil majors into beginning to even consider delivering the stranded gas that they've been sitting on in the form of untapped leases. I don't know why anyone would think that they now have our best interests at heart when it comes to bringing this badly needed domestic energy to market. Bringing the gas overland through Canada is a bad idea. I've said it before, more than once, and now the reasons . . . are even more than self-evident. It is time to shift course and protect our own interests. Along the way, we can reduce our dependence on foreign energy, make a sizable dent in the trade deficit, jumpstart a foundering economy and revitalize the domestic waterfront. Or, we can build a pipeline in Canada.

6

The Alaska Gas Pipeline Could Be an Ecological Disaster

Abby Schultz

Abby Schultz has written about environmental issues and business for publications including the New York Times *and* CRO: Corporate Responsibility Officer.

Even though natural gas is often hailed as a more environmentally friendly alternative to oil, environmentalists fear that much of the natural gas from the proposed Alaska gas pipeline—which would run through Canada—would be used for Canadian tar sands operations, the conversion of a mixture of clay, sand, and a tar-like form of petroleum into crude oil. These operations devour not only a lot of energy, but also produce oil that creates more greenhouse gas emissions than regular crude oil. Furthermore, natural gas supplies available for the tar sand operations have been declining, and Canada will need Alaskan gas to keep the production of oil profitable. In light of recent discoveries of large gas reserves in the United States, an Alaskan gas pipeline might be of little use for the American market and merely help Canada continue an environmentally hazardous form of oil production.

Where the natural gas from the Alaska Natural Gas Pipeline will end up is a murky question tied up in a 30-year-old treaty, expansion of Canadian tar sands [a mixture of clay, sand and bitumen, a tar-like form of petroleum] operations and trends in natural gas supplies both in the United States and in Canada.

Environmentalists fear at least half of the relatively clean-burning Alaskan North Slope gas will end up fueling tar sands operations in Alberta, where the pipeline will end, instead of coming to the Lower 48 [contiguous] states to replace carbon-intensive coal in power plants. The tar sands operations already consume about 20 percent of Canada's natural gas, and they are expected to need as much as twice that by 2035.

Michael Brune of the Rainforest Action Network calls the pipeline "a stealth dirty oil mega-project . . . conceived by Big Oil."

"Under Plan Palin, ExxonMobil and TransCanada would construct a 1,700-mile natural gas pipeline from the Arctic, heading south," Brune writes. "About half of it is likely to be siphoned to help produce the dirtiest oil on earth."

It might not be that simple, though.

Dividing Up the Gas

Where the natural gas ends up may depend on a 1977 treaty between the U.S. and Canada that would require gas equal to the amount produced in Alaska be exported to the Lower 48.

The 1,700-mile pipeline, which appears to be moving forward more than 40 years after 100 trillion cubic feet of natural gas was discovered in the Alaskan North Slope, is viewed by policy makers as a way to boost domestic production of a relatively clean fuel at a time the U.S. is trying to move to a cleaner energy economy and to wean itself off foreign sources of oil.

In February [2009], President [Barack] Obama told the *Anchorage Daily News* that the pipeline was "promising" as a national energy source.

But nongovernmental organizations, including the Rainforest Action Network and Corporate Ethics International, expect at least half the natural gas flowing through the pipeline will remain [in] Alberta, where the pipeline ends, rather [than] shifting to other pipelines bound for the Lower 48. That's because Alberta is home to most of Canada's tar sands operations, which rely heavily on natural gas to mine, process and upgrade sticky, thick bitumen into synthetic crude oil.

Converting tar sands, a mixture of clay, sand and bitumen, into oil creates 5 percent to 15 percent more greenhouse gas emissions than the average crude oil, according to IHS Cambridge Energy Research Associates [CERA].

Tar sands production is also associated with a host of environmental problems, including the mining of pristine Boreal forests [Taiga, characterized by conifer forests] and the creation of huge "tailings ponds" filled with toxic materials. Environmentalists call tar sands a "dirty" fuel and note the irony of using natural gas in its production.

"While natural gas is a little cleaner than oil, if it's being used to produce dirty oil, it just doesn't make sense," says Kenny Bruno, campaign coordinator at Corporate Ethics.

Financing for the pipeline may rest on how much Alaska gas reaches the Lower 48.

U.S.-Canada Treaties

One factor in whether the gas makes it to the Lower 48 may depend on interpretation of a 1977 treaty between the U.S. and Canada that was a precursor to the Northern Pipelines Act. The treaty guarantees "whatever volume of gas comes from Alaska must result in an equal volume being exported," says Joseph Balash, intergovernmental coordinator to Alaska Governor Sarah Palin.

The principles of the treaty, however, may not apply, given that the treaty was written more than 30 years ago and a different pipeline is now under consideration. The U.S. State Department will make that determination.

"It may be that the treaty needs to be slightly amended, completely revised, or thrown out altogether. It's a matter of whether or not they want to make the existing agreement work or not," Balash says.

Mark Myers, coordinator of the Alaska Gasline Inducement Act [AGIA] for the state of Alaska, doesn't believe the treaty in the end will have much of an impact, and that even if consumption by the tar sands industry increases and gas supplies decline, there will be plenty of gas to export the 4.5 billion cubic feet a day to the lower 48 states the Alaska gas pipeline is expected to deliver. The AGIA was passed by the Alaska legislature in 2007 to spur construction of the pipeline.

"I still believe 15 to 20 years from now there will be a significant amount of export to the U.S.," Myers says. "It may not be as much as today, but it will be more than 4.5 billion cubic feet."

The Influence of Federal Financing

Financing for the pipeline may rest on how much Alaska gas reaches the Lower 48.

The Natural Gas Pipeline Act of 2004 provides about $18 billion in loan guarantees for pipeline construction, in addition to tax incentives. These dollars won't be insignificant for a project estimated to cost between $26 billion and $40 billion. A report written by the Congressional Research Service in September 2008 points out that the rationale for federal support of the pipeline was to increase the supply of natural gas to the lower 48 states. In other words, federal dollars could be in jeopardy if the pipeline doesn't serve the U.S.

"There is a potential for misunderstanding if Canadian exports to the United States decrease as Alaska natural gas arrives," the report says.

TransCanada, which received a license under AGIA last August [2008] to build the pipeline, and Balash in Gov. Palin's office both note that Canada has shipped surplus gas to the

U.S. for years and that there's no reason to expect that will change. Once the pipeline is operational in 10 years, TransCanada says it will increase the available gas in the market without a consequential change in Canadian demand.

"Therefore we would expect that the entire Alaskan volumes will ultimately be consumed in the Lower 48 since Canada will continue to have surplus gas," says Terry Cunha, a TransCanada spokesman.

But the picture for natural gas supplies in Alberta isn't that clear.

There are two big factors at work. First, increased demands from the energy-intensive oil sands industry. Second, tighter future supplies of natural gas in the region.

The pace of growth in the oil sands industry will be affected by oil prices, oil supplies, the health of the economy and greenhouse gas regulation. Estimates range for oil sands production to increase from about 1.2 million barrels a day in 2006 to as high as 4.3 million barrels a day by 2030, according to the U.S. Energy Information Administration's latest Annual Energy Outlook.

Conventional supplies of natural gas in Alberta peaked in about 2001 and have been on the decline since, [says] Bob Dunbar of Strategy West, a consulting firm in Calgary, Alberta, focused on the oil sands industry.

Another factor in the bleaker future for conventional Canadian natural gas supplies reaching the tar sands is a proposed pipeline called Mackenzie Valley, which would bring gas from the Canadian Arctic to Alberta, but is stalled in regulatory limbo.

The Congressional Research Service also notes [that] it's unclear whether "there is adequate, large diameter pipe reduction capacity in the entire world to serve both Alaska and Mackenzie Valley projects at the same time," and that supporters of the Mackenzie project fear the economics of the pipeline won't work if the Alaska project is finished first.

The Pipeline Route

The 1,700-mile pipeline proposed by TransCanada will begin in Prudhoe Bay in the North Slope of Alaska and will parallel the existing trans-Alaska oil pipeline to Delta Junction, south of Fairbanks, where it will then follow the Alaska Highway, continuing through northern British Columbia to link with the Alberta Hub on TransCanada's pipeline grid in northwestern Alberta.

It is expected initially to carry an average of 4.5 billion cubic feet of natural gas a day, or 1,600 billion cubic feet a year.

"Once gas is into that system, the molecules of gas aren't segregated in any way," Dunbar says. "It becomes part of the overall North American Gas Transmission Network."

Tar sands operations consume 20 percent of Canada's natural gas, according [to] IHS-CERA.

To direct natural gas only to the U.S., a separate pipeline would be needed, Dunbar says.

[A] $30 billion, 2,000-mile-long project to bring Alaska North Slope gas to the Lower 48 called Denali-The Alaska Gas Pipeline is [also] planned by BP and ConocoPhillips, but it too would go through Alberta. Both projects are holding a so-called open season in 2010 where producers bid to provide gas to the pipeline. If the open season is successful for Denali, the project will file with the Federal Energy Regulatory Commission in the U.S. and the National Energy Board in Canada to build the pipeline.

Tar sands operations consume 20 percent of Canada's natural gas, according [to] IHS-CERA. By 2035, it says, tar sands operations could consume 25 percent to 40 percent of Canada's natural gas.

Canada's Own Natural Gas Reserves

In a June [2009] report on Alberta's energy reserves, the Alberta Energy Research Conservation Board [ERCB] said 360 billion cubic feet of natural gas were purchased for the oil sands operations in 2008. Those purchases are expected to climb to about 830 billion cubic feet by 2018, the Alberta ERCB said. That's half the 1,600 billion cubic feet a day that would flow through the pipeline beginning about 2018.

In the same time period, Alberta expects to continue exporting natural gas, but the estimated amount available for export will decline from about 3 trillion cubic feet in 2008 to 1.37 trillion cubic feet in 2018, according to the ERCB.

While supplies of Canadian natural gas may be plateauing or on the decline, the oil sands industry expects [that] greater efficiencies in production, as well as new sources of fuel, could reduce the industry's demand on purchased natural gas.

However, the new sources of fuel include gasification of petroleum coke and asphaltenes, which are the bottom-of-the-barrel deposits of the bitumen left after processing it into synthetic crude. These technologies are more carbon intensive than natural gas, and the industry is already under pressure to reduce its carbon footprint, according to Dan Woynillowicz of the Pembina Institute.

"Switching to any of those fuels will make producing a barrel of oil sands even dirtier," Woynillowicz says.

Dunbar notes that it's easier to capture the carbon dioxide emitted from gasification, rather than [to burn] natural gas, but Woynillowicz points out the carbon capture and storage remains an untested, expensive technology.

[Although] demand is increasing, and supplies of Canadian gas may be dwindling, there are a couple more factors at work. One is that gas supplies in the U.S. are likely to expand from unconventional sources of natural gas, mainly from shale, which would reduce demand in the lower 48 states for Alaskan natural gas. Like tar sands, however, unconventional sources of gas from shale and coal bed methane are more carbon intensive to produce, and [they] have other environmental consequences, such as heavy water use in the case of shale extraction.

"Fundamentally this is why we are coming back to the overarching notion that we need to accelerate the transition away from fossil fuels for both economic and environmental reasons, because we're getting into the dirtiest fossil fuels to extract," Woynillowicz says.

7

The Alaska Natural Gas Pipeline Can Be Built and Operated Safely

Rod Combellick

Rod Combellick is deputy director of the Alaska Department of Natural Resources' Division of Geological & Geophysical Surveys.

Alaska records a large number of earthquakes every day. Any proposed pipeline bringing gas from the North Slope through Canada to the contiguous United States must take into account geologic and seismic data and be constructed in such a way that it can withstand earthquakes in difficult and nearly inaccessible terrain. The Trans-Alaska Pipeline, which withstood an earthquake in 2002, has shown that current technology is up to this task. If developers rely on expertise acquired in past years, a natural gas pipeline can be installed successfully.

With 50 to 100 earthquakes recorded daily, including an average of one magnitude-7 event every year and a magnitude-8 or larger event every 13 years, Alaska is by far the most seismically active region in North America. The 1964 magnitude-9.2 earthquake in southern Alaska slightly edges out the December 2004 northern Sumatra event as the second largest earthquake ever recorded. As a result of its seismicity, parts of Alaska pose formidable challenges for designing and building structures to safely withstand earthquake forces and seismically induced ground failures.

Rod Combellick, "Building a Natural Gas Pipeline Through Earthquake Country," *Geotimes*, November 2006. Copyright © 2006 the American Geological Institute. Reproduced by permission.

Alaska is also rich in natural resources, including oil and natural gas, producing about 928,500 barrels of oil daily, or 20 percent of all U.S. production in 2005. So the question then becomes: Can a pipeline intended to carry critically important commodities for many decades be safely built and operated across such a seismically active region?

Mastering Pipeline Construction

This question was answered Nov. 3, 2002, when the Denali Fault in central Alaska slipped approximately 5.5 meters (18 feet) laterally and more than 1 meter (3 feet) vertically beneath the Trans-Alaska Pipeline during a magnitude-7.9 earthquake without causing a single drop of oil to spill. Although no significant historic earthquakes had previously been attributed to the Denali Fault, geologists during the early 1970s recognized the fault's earthquake potential and recommended a design along a 600-meter section to accommodate slippage up to 6 meters in a magnitude-8 earthquake.

The event the geologists forecasted occurred 30 years later. (In geologic studies following the earthquake, tree-ring evidence showed that a magnitude-7.2 earthquake in 1912 had occurred along the same trace of the fault.) Engineers accommodated the predicted ground motion by incorporating a zig-zag design supported on Teflon sliders, allowing the pipe to flex and the ground to slide beneath it.

Because of the economic and logistical hurdles, natural gas on the North Slope has been considered "stranded."

With proposals now being considered to build a natural gas pipeline, it is ever-important to understand the seismic hazards along potential routes, so that the pipeline and its spurs can be properly designed and managed for seismic safety. Many variables will surely play into the construction of the natural gas transporter; fortunately, earth scientists already know much about the geology and seismology of the region, and they have learned much more in the 30 years since the oil pipeline's construction.

On the Table

Until now, getting any of the estimated 35 trillion cubic feet of proven natural gas reserves on the North Slope to market has been considered uneconomic due to the remoteness of the area, relatively low commodity prices and high costs of suitable transportation. Therefore, nearly all of the natural gas that is produced from oil wells in the Prudhoe Bay area is reinjected [into a subterranean reservoir already containing natural gas or gas and crude oil] for storage and to help maintain reservoir pressures for oil recovery.

Because of the economic and logistical hurdles, natural gas on the North Slope has been considered "stranded." Rising energy prices and recent shortages of heating fuel across the United States, however, have sparked renewed interest in marketing this stranded gas and developing new domestic gas sources. North Slope oil producers and other companies are stepping up their exploration for new gas reserves. The state of Alaska is also keenly interested in getting the gas to market because of the significant potential revenue it will bring to the state in the form of taxes and royalties. In addition, a pipeline through Alaska could provide affordable energy for homes and businesses in local communities.

The state of Alaska has received three formal proposals for construction of a pipeline and possible spur lines to deliver natural gas from the North Slope to U.S. and world markets. A fourth, "over-the-top," alternate route involves a submerged pipeline extending from Prudhoe Bay eastward through the Beaufort Sea to Canada's Mackenzie Delta, but is opposed by the state of Alaska and Congress and is not under consideration.

Two of the proposals under consideration follow the same route, paralleling the existing Alaskan oil pipeline for approximately 880 kilometers from Prudhoe Bay to Delta Junction, then turning southeast and following the Alaska Highway to a hub in Alberta, Canada. In the third proposal, the gas pipeline would follow the oil pipeline for its entire length to a liquefied natural gas plant near Valdez, where the liquid gas would be transferred to ships for export.

All of these proposals allow for the pipeline to be tapped for delivery of gas to Alaska communities via various spur lines. The routes these spur lines take will have great bearing on the pipeline system's exposure to seismic hazards.

Hazard Evaluation

Earthquake hazards do not currently compete with economic and political factors in selection of a pipeline route, but [they] will figure prominently into the design and engineering once the route has been determined. If the gas pipeline follows the route of the oil pipeline for its entire route from Prudhoe Bay to Valdez, the seismic hazards to which it is exposed will be similar. A key difference, however, is that in current proposals the entire gas pipeline will be buried to avoid explosions from accidents or sabotage.

An additional risk could come from soil liquefying during an earthquake.

Clearly, innovative engineering will be necessary where the gas pipeline crosses active faults, including possibly elevating the line, or placing it in aboveground embankments or in specially designed trenches in those zones. A separate but significant hazard will be the effect of permafrost and frost ... on the gas line, especially in light of the opinion of many scientists that global warming will raise temperatures enough to melt ground ice in some areas during the coming decades.

All of the proposed gas pipeline routes cross active seismic zones in the Fairbanks region north of the Denali Fault, though none of these zones are associated with mapped surface fault traces. Surprisingly, three shallow magnitude-7-plus earthquakes have shaken the area within 80 kilometers of Fairbanks during the past century with no discernable surface rupture so far. Most earthquakes in this area are associated with zones of seismicity that line up in a northeast-southwest direction between the Denali and Tintina-Kaltag fault systems.

If the gas pipeline follows the Alaska Highway from Delta Junction into Canada, as proposed in two of the plans, it will cross additional northeast-trending faults. This part of the route is an area of relatively low seismicity; however, published and unpublished geologic studies have identified several northeast-trending faults north and south of the corridor, and faults along the northeast front of the Alaska Range mountains adjacent to the corridor, with known or suspected geologically recent activity. Some of the northeast-trending faults may be continuous across the pipeline route.

Soil "Liquefaction"

Continuing along the two plans' route to Canada, an additional risk could come from soil liquefying during an earthquake. Such "liquefaction" can cause an improperly designed pipeline to rise bouyantly, as it may be lighter than the surrounding soil, creating stresses that could cause the pipes to crack or break. Lateral spreading or flowage of the soil, which are common consequences of liquefaction on sloping ground, could also break the pipeline. Liquefaction was extensive in lowlands between Tok and the Alaska-Canada border during the 2002 Denali Fault earthquake, causing extensive damage to roads and an airport runway.

If the gas pipeline continues along the Alaska Highway through Canada, it will follow the Denali Fault trench for about 200 kilometers in southwestern Yukon before turning eastward toward Whitehorse. This portion of the Denali Fault shows extensive evidence of geologically recent activity and could pose significant seismic risk; however, the 2002 rupture took a turn southward along a splay called the Totschunda Fault rather than following the main strand into Canada. Whether future activity on this part of the system will return to the Denali Fault or shift to the Totschunda and other faults to the southwest is not known.

With 600 to 700 years since the last significant offset, the Castle Mountain Fault may be due for a magnitude-6 to [magnitude]-7 event.

The alternative, third, route to Valdez crosses the Denali Fault, like the oil pipeline, and crosses the smaller Donnelly Dome and McGinnis Glacier faults in the Alaska Range north of the Denali Fault. Additionally, where the pipeline approaches its southern terminus in Valdez, the pipeline and proposed liquefied natural gas plant would be subject to potentially very strong ground shaking from large earthquakes in the Alaska-Aleutian subduction zone—the source of the 1964 magnitude-9.2 earthquake.

Additional Considerations

Also important to consider are proposed spur lines from Fairbanks and Glennallen to the Anchorage area, which will traverse highly seismically active regions, with most historic earthquakes originating in the Benioff zone of the Alaska-Aleutian megathrust. In addition to the Denali Fault, a pipeline from Fairbanks to Anchorage along the Parks Highway would cross the Castle Mountain Fault in the lower Susitna River Valley. About 50 kilometers east of the highway, this fault was the source of a magnitude-5.7 earthquake in 1984 and a magnitude-4.6 earthquake in 1996, although neither resulted in recognized surface rupture.

In its currently aseismic western section near the Parks Highway, the Castle Mountain Fault shows clear evidence of geologically recent activity. Paleoseismic studies [which focus on the timing, location, and size of prehistoric earthquakes] there suggest evidence of four prehistoric earthquakes in the past 2,700 years, indicating an average recurrence interval of about 700 years. With 600 to 700 years since the last significant offset, the Castle Mountain Fault may be due for a magnitude-6 to [magnitude]-7 event.

Recent studies also suggest the presence of a fold-and-thrust fault belt with possible recent activity in [the] foothills of the Alaska Range north of the Denali Fault. This finding could mean that the risk to spur lines crossing the Alaska Range in this area is higher than previously thought. And although a spur line from Glennallen to Anchorage would not cross known active faults, it would be subject to ground shaking from subduction-zone events, and it comes into close proximity to the Castle Mountain Fault.

Mapping Efforts

To better understand the geologic hazards along the proposed gas pipeline corridor for two of the proposals, the Alaska Division of Geological & Geophysical Surveys (DGGS) initiated a study in 2005 of geologic hazards along the 300-kilometer segment between Delta Junction and the Alaska-Canada border. This study includes detailed geologic mapping of a 20-kilometer-wide swath along the corridor, as well as fault studies in and near the corridor to evaluate seismic and other hazards. In addition, the Department of Mining and Geological Engineering at the University of Alaska in Fairbanks is compiling data on the geology and hazards in Canada for a proposed extension of the Alaska Railroad along the same corridor.

DGGS conducted a high-resolution airborne geophysical survey in 2005 to aid the geologic mapping in this area of extensive vegetation and soil cover and to help determine whether suspected active fault zones are continuous across the corridor. Preliminary interpretation of the geophysical data indicates that at least one of the fault zones extends more than 25 kilometers across the corridor, although there is no evidence yet of geologically recent activity. This fault zone, as well as others, will be the focus of studies over the next two to three years to determine slip rates and the age of the most recent displacement.

When DGGS completes its evaluation, the relative seismic risk of the route between Delta Junction and the Alaska-Canada border can be determined and the pipeline designed accordingly, if it takes this route. Meanwhile, although that portion of the proposed pipeline traverses an area of low seismicity, it does not necessarily translate to low risk; seismicity along the Denali Fault was very low prior to the 2002 event.

Clearly, the presence of faults with evidence of geologically recent offset in and near this corridor justifies increasing the number of seismic instruments there and collecting detailed geologic data. Furthermore, if the pipeline continues to follow the Alaska Highway through Canada, its design must take into account probable high seismic hazards for the portion of this route that would follow the Denali Fault in southwestern Yukon.

Seismic Risks

Perhaps the greatest seismic risk posed, however, is to the proposed spur pipeline route along the Parks Highway from Fairbanks to Anchorage because it crosses portions of the Denali and Castle Mountain faults that appear overdue for an earthquake, as well as a belt of possibly active thrust faults along the foothills of the Alaska Range north of the Denali Fault. A recent GPS survey along the Parks Highway shows that [seismic] strain is accumulating across that section of the Denali Fault zone at a rate comparable to that of the section that ruptured in 2002. This strain could be released in an earthquake any time in the next few years, decades or even centuries.

A gas pipeline that follows the existing oil pipeline to Valdez also has some risk, as it crosses the portion of the Denali Fault that ruptured in 2002 and would terminate in the rupture area of the 1964 earthquake. Because significant strain already has been released, however, the risk from repeats of these earthquakes is probably low for the operational lifetime of the oil and gas pipelines.

Still, designs should accommodate the possibility of similar events and utilize all available data on other earthquake sources along the route. The 1964 and 2002 events provided valuable engineering data, including probable upper bounds on ground-shaking forces and fault offsets to be expected from earthquakes on those source zones.

In the end, regardless of the route selected for the proposed Alaska natural gas pipeline, seismic hazards will be a major consideration in design, construction and operation. As demonstrated by the successful performance of the Trans-Alaska Pipeline during the 2002 Denali Fault earthquake, however, seismic safety is possible even in one of the most seismically active areas of the world. Building and operating pipelines safely in earthquake country depends on acquisition of reliable geologic and seismic data, and the proper use of those data in design and construction.

8

Natural Gas Can Contribute to Clean Energy Objectives

Robert Bryce

Robert Bryce has written for numerous publications, including Atlantic Monthly, Slate, American Conservative, *the* Wall Street Journal, *the* Washington Post, *and the* Guardian. *He is the author of* Gusher of Lies: The Dangerous Delusion of "Energy Independence."

The United States has discovered new, enormous natural gas reserves, but the good news is tempered by falling gas prices, which make it unprofitable for developers to extract the gas. If the government is serious about reducing greenhouse gas emissions, it should implement a carbon tax, which would help raise the demand for natural gas. Only then will the production of natural gas increase.

The collapse in oil prices gets most of the headlines. But the corresponding collapse in natural gas prices may be the more important story for both the short- and long-term interests of the U.S.

On July 1 [2008], natural gas futures peaked at $13.51. On July 14, crude oil futures peaked at $145.16 per barrel. Today [December 11, 2008], the spot price for natural gas is about $5.67 and the spot price for oil is about $46. And those prices may go lower still. On November 24 [2008], Jen Snyder, the head of North American gas research for the energy consult-

Robert Bryce, "It's a Gas, Gas, Gas: The Paradigm Shift in the U.S. Natural Gas Business," EnergyTribune.com, December 11, 2008. Reproduced by permission.

ing firm Wood Mackenzie, released a report [in] which she claimed that the U.S. gas market should expect to see natural gas prices "in the range of $5 to $6" for the next five years.

A Natural Gas Slowdown Is Looming

While many analysts have discounted Snyder's prediction, the potential for a long-term slowdown in natural gas drilling in the U.S. could have devastating effects on the drillers and oil-field service companies. The . . . rigs drilling for gas usually outnumber those looking for oil by more than 3 to 1. But now that the U.S. is awash in gas, a drastic slowdown in drilling has begun. That can be seen by looking at the latest rig count numbers from [oil field services company] Baker Hughes. And Texas, the biggest natural gas producer in the country, provides a good barometer for the trend. In September [2008], an average of 946 rigs were working in the Lone Star State. By the first week in December [2008], the number of active rigs in Texas had fallen to 852.

The bear market in gas will be exacerbated by recent announcements. Yesterday [December 10, 2008], Houston-based Petrohawk Energy announced that three of its new wells in the Haynesville Shale in Louisiana were each producing more than 20 million cubic feet of gas per day. Those are the biggest wells ever recorded in Petrohawk's history. Also yesterday, Dallas-based Exco Resources announced its own Haynesville well, which was also flowing gas at more than 20 MMcf/d [million cubic feet per day].

Those are sizable wells by any measure. Keep in mind that the U.S. produces about 19.2 billion cubic feet of gas per day from more than 448,000 wells. That means that the average U.S. gas well produces about 43,000 cubic feet per day. These new Haynesville wells are showing initial production rates that are three orders of magnitude larger than that. And those new wells are coming online at the same time that some gas producers in Oklahoma have shut in [closed] their wells rather than sell their gas at current prices. Furthermore, some 2 billion cubic feet of daily gas production in the Gulf of Mexico continues to be shut in due to lingering damage from this summer's [2008]hurricanes.

Huge Resources Are Available

The new reality for the gas industry is one of enormous available resources, with much [of] that availability coming from the new shale plays like the Haynesville, Fayetteville, and Marcellus. In July [2008], a study done by Navigant Consulting estimated that America's potential gas resources may total 2,200 trillion cubic feet. That's 50 percent more gas than the current proven reserves of Russia and twice as much as the proven reserves in Iran. Put into oil terms, that 2,200 Tcf [trillion cubic feet] of gas is the equivalent of one-and-a-half Saudi Arabias. A more recent study, published in mid-November [2008] by consulting firm ICF International, estimated U.S. gas resources at 1,830 trillion cubic feet. In petroleum terms, that's the oil equivalent of 329 billion barrels of oil or about three Kuwaits.

On November 11 [2008], during a meeting of the Independent Petroleum Association of America [IPAA] held in Houston, Mark Papa, the chairman and CEO of EOG Resources, said the U.S. gas industry was in the midst of a "total sea change unlike anything we've seen in our careers. Don't underestimate the power of that sea change." Papa said that the Haynesville Shale, which may contain 50 trillion cubic feet of gas, the equivalent of about 9 billion barrels of oil, is one of "the biggest fields found in the entire world over the last decade." At that size, the Haynesville field would be bigger than the massive offshore Tupi discovery in Brazil that was announced by Petrobras in 2007. Papa said that the shale gas deposits provide a "huge amount of gas that can be mined. And I use the term 'mined' because the geologic risk has been minimized."

Although the geologic risk has been minimized, other risks have come to the fore. Fifteen years ago, natural gas was "hard to find and easy to produce," says David Pursell, a managing director at Tudor, Pickering, Holt & Co., a Houston-based investment banking firm. With these new shale plays, gas is "easy to find and hard to produce. . . . You have traded one risk for another." In the past, the U.S. gas business was focused on geology and geophysics. Now, says Pursell, "It's much more of a completion and engineering game."

The problem for the gas industry is a familiar one: profits.

Indeed, the ability of natural gas producers to get big production numbers from their shale wells requires them to employ multiple hydraulic fractures in a single well. The Exco well announced yesterday [December 10, 2008] had a nine-stage fracture [injection of a liquid into a well to aid in extraction] on a horizontal lateral [drilling sideways into a formation] that was 4,481 feet long.

Pete Stark, the vice president of industry relations at IHS, a Denver-based data and consulting firm, says these new shale plays are "an incredible plus for U.S. energy security." But he adds that the negative for the gas companies and gas drillers is that this "huge supply growth is coming onstream at the same time that demand is falling out of bed. So it's a killer for the industry going forward."

Thus, the problem for the gas industry is a familiar one: profits. During their discussion at the IPAA meeting in Houston, Papa of EOG Resources and Jeff Wojahn of EnCana said that their companies needed natural gas prices to be in the $7 to $8 range for their shale drilling programs to be profitable. Obviously, given current prices, all of the gas-focused independent companies are scaling back their drilling programs by as much as 50 percent. And it's not yet apparent how many drilling rigs will be idled in the coming months as more and more companies slash their capital expenditure budgets.

H.G. "Buddy" Kleemeier, the president and CEO of Tulsa-based Kaiser-Francis Oil Company, says that the gas industry must adapt to this new paradigm: huge available resources, minimized geologic risk, increased engineering risks, and on-going price risk. In the past, the oil and gas industry was largely regulated by either government restrictions on production (prorationing that was administered by the Texas Railroad Commission) or restrictions on how gas could be used (like the Powerplant and Industrial Fuel Use Act of 1978) or by pricing regimes imposed by regulators.

The irony is that the current excess of domestic natural gas is bad news for the very industry that made the gas glut possible.

Today, the natural gas industry operates in a largely deregulated environment. Given that fact, Kleemeier (who is also the current chairman of the IPAA) expects the gas industry to be governed by what he calls "prorationing by price." When prices fall, drilling rigs will be idled. And those rigs will remain idle until prices recover.

Too Many Resources

Obviously, the U.S. will need to keep drilling lots of new wells as these shale gas wells have steep decline curves. But it will take many months, or perhaps several years, before the U.S. gas industry understands the optimal rate of drilling. The hard truth about the current gas glut is that the U.S. gas industry has been victimized by its own success. The amazing technological breakthroughs in extracting natural gas from shale has led to a surfeit [superabundance] of gas. At the IPAA meeting last month [November 2008], Porter Bennett, the president and CEO of Bentek Energy, an Evergreen,

Colorado-based consulting firm, said, "We have more gas than we know what to do with." That's good news for consumers. It's good news for the environment, as increased natural gas use should result in cleaner air. And more natural gas use in the truck and car fleet could help reduce U.S. oil consumption.

The irony is that the current excess of domestic natural gas is bad news for the very industry that made the gas glut possible. And now, the gas industry must look to the new [President Barack] Obama administration for some type of legislation that could help spur natural gas demand and therefore raise prices. That legislation could come in the form of a tax on carbon or more restrictions on coal-fired power plants. For Stark, the policy path should be obvious: "If the Obama administration is at all clever, they will capitalize on this increased gas production and use it to solve quite a few clean-energy objectives for the country."

9

Natural Gas Might Not Free America from Foreign Energy

Thomas Grose

Thomas Grose is a writer based in London, England.

Natural gas is getting good press as an abundant and clean energy source, yet it might not be a cheap alternative to crude oil. Gas reserves are limited, prices are usually moving in tandem with oil, and global gas demand will increase and bring about shortages and high prices. Furthermore, the U.S. market is geared toward oil consumption and it will be hard and expensive to retrofit cars and gas stations to accommodate natural gas. In light of a multitude of challenges, the future of natural gas and its potential to change the country's dependence on oil is not encouraging.

Natural gas is the only fossil fuel capable of getting good press these days. Its fans regularly rhapsodize about its merits, calling it an extraordinary fuel that's cheap, domestically abundant, and clean. Well, cleaner than oil, at least. Meanwhile, everyone from Texas oilman T. Boone Pickens to the Sierra Club is promoting natural gas as the key that America needs to free itself from its century-long addiction to oil. After all, the nation's appetite for oil means that nearly 60 percent of the petroleum consumed each year must be imported, much of it from unstable or unsavory regimes in the Middle East, Africa, and Latin America.

Pickens, along with a growing number of groups, wants America to slash its oil consumption by making better use of natural gas. In theory, the plan sounds simple. Around 22 percent of the natural gas burned each year is used to generate electricity. If wind energy were substituted for gas at power plants, the freed-up natural gas could be used instead to fuel ground transportation systems, starting with diesel-burning fleet trucks and buses. Advocates say this plan could cut U.S. oil imports by up to 38 percent.

Uncertain Consequences

Yet if the nation makes the switch from oil to natural gas to run its vehicles, will it simply be trading one foreign-dependent fuel for another? The answer is, probably. But to what extent is very hard to say. "Welcome to uncertainty," says Gordon Kaufman, a professor emeritus and oil and gas expert at the Massachusetts Institute of Technology's Sloan School of Management.

Currently, only 16 percent of the natural gas America consumes is imported. That's much better than oil, of course, but it doesn't eliminate foreign supplies. And while most of what is imported today comes from Canada by pipeline, Canada is increasingly using more of its gas domestically. That means any expansion in U.S. demand would almost certainly have to draw upon other foreign sources, which would ship it to U.S. ports as liquefied natural gas, or LNG.

Russian roulette. It's not encouraging to look at where the Earth's concentrations of natural gas lie. Three countries have more than 55 percent of the world's proven reserves: Russia (25.2 percent), Iran (15.7 percent), and Qatar (14.4 percent). Other countries that have fairly substantial reserves include Saudi Arabia, the United Arab Emirates, Nigeria, and Algeria. "It is hardly politically a smart move to rely on these countries for supplies," notes Martin Blunt, a professor of petroleum engineering at London's Imperial College. Russia, for instance, has twice used its gas resources as a political weapon by turning off supplies to its European neighbors, most recently last winter [2008].

Moreover, even if U.S. companies wanted to buy Russian gas, not much would be available in the short term. While Russia pipes a lot of gas to Europe, it hasn't gotten heavily involved in the LNG market so far.

The Future of Gas Is Unclear

Natural gas is also gaining in popularity worldwide. Global consumption could increase more than twofold in coming years, and that could make for a very competitive and unreliable international market. Exporting countries will ship gas to wherever they can get the best price. And countries like Japan and South Korea, which are much more reliant upon imports than the United States, have shown a willingness to pay top dollar. Japan imports more than four times as much LNG as the United States, while South Korea imports nearly 58 percent more. "We would be competing with everyone," says Steve Gabriel, an expert on natural gas markets at Resources for the Future. "If we have to get into the international market, we might have a problem."

So, what about those bountiful domestic supplies that proponents talk about? Can they free the country from the clutches of foreign suppliers? Perhaps, but probably not entirely. The Energy Information Administration [EIA] says that U.S. dependence on foreign natural gas could drop from 16 percent to 3 percent by 2030 if it takes full advantage of so-far untapped reserves. That would include tapping unconventional sources, mainly from shale, opening up Alaska's gas fields, and mining the gas beneath the ocean along the outer continental shelf.

"But those are big 'ifs,'" says David Pumphrey, deputy director of the energy program at the Center for Strategic and International Studies. For instance, there's a fair amount of political and environmental opposition to going after the Alaskan and OCS [outer continental shelf] gas. Some are worried, for example, that an Alaskan pipeline could damage Arctic permafrost.

Shale gas may be the easiest and least controversial of these resources to mine. But it has only been in recent years that new technology—a form of horizontal drilling initially perfected and used to great success in the Barrett shale of north Texas—has made shale gas accessible. Accordingly, estimates of the size of U.S. shale gas deposits are rising. The Potential Gas Committee, an independent U.S. body of energy experts, delivers its biennial report on U.S. gas reserves in April [2009]; it says it expects to note that there has been "a significant increase in technically recoverable shale gas resources."

Mining Difficulties

Still, even the rosiest scenarios could be tripped up by cost. Mining unconventional gas is a much more expensive proposition than releasing it from traditional sources. "There's definitely a lot of gas in the ground," says Tony Meggs, BP's recently retired group vice president for research and technology. "The issue is not whether it's there as much as whether you can get it out at any reasonable cost."

Here's the quandary: If natural gas prices are low enough to make it an attractive alternative to consumers, it may not be financially worthwhile to extract the hard-to-get stuff from shale or the seas. Last summer [2008], natural gas was selling for around $14 per million British thermal units; by December, the price was under $6. The result? In December 2008, there were 400 fewer gas rigs operating in the United States than six months earlier. It's also difficult to argue that natural gas is a cheaper alternative to oil, because its price tends to move in tandem with oil prices. And when the price of gas occasionally decouples itself from oil, that's not necessarily a good thing. "Its price is often more volatile than oil's," Pumphrey says.

The cost of converting a gasoline car to natural gas ranges from $12,500 to $22,500.

Power Switch. Even if the economics and technologies of extraction somehow converge to produce a plentiful supply, it would be difficult and costly for the United States to switch from gasoline to natural gas to power automobiles. Gasoline's retail infrastructure is as convenient as it is efficient, and most Americans are never very far from a filling station. Building a new and just-as-easy-to-use natural-gas retail distribution system from scratch would cost billions of dollars, and it's not clear who would pay for it, particularly if there are doubts about consumer demand. "That's something I can't get my arms around," admits Melanie Kenderdine, an associate director at MIT's Energy Initiative. "If you can't, to a maximum extent, use the existing infrastructure, you will run into enormous resistance."

For a switch to work fully and extend beyond truck and bus fleets, it would also require millions of consumers to convert their cars to run on natural gas instead of gasoline. The time, effort, and cost it would take for manufacturers to make—and for consumers to buy—a new breed of car that's affordable would be enormous, even if automakers were willing to produce it. The only natural-gas car on the market today, the Honda Civic GX, is hardly a bargain. It has a sticker price of $25,190—nearly $10,000 more than a normal Civic— and can travel only 170 miles on a tank of fuel.

Costs Might Prove Prohibitive

Pricey. Can millions of consumers be persuaded to retrofit their cars? The cost of converting a gasoline car to natural gas ranges from $12,500 to $ 22,500. That's pretty expensive, even though 50 to 80 percent of the cost can be offset by federal tax credits. And, in fact, only a handful of large sedans, pickups, and passenger vans currently are capable of being retrofitted. Meanwhile, a gallon equivalent of compressed natural gas at the pump is less than a dollar cheaper than a gallon of gasoline. That's not the kind of price break likely to compel many people to make such a big upfront investment. "When oil was $140 a barrel, a lot of things that looked economical then no longer look so economical now," Gabriel says. Of course, many oil experts say that once the recession ends, oil prices will skyrocket once again; the EIA predicts a barrel of oil will sell for $189 by 2030.

Nevertheless, many believe that natural gas remains better suited to generating electricity than powering trucks and cars. For one thing, BP's Meggs notes, producing electricity more cleanly should be a higher priority. Globally, 40 percent of carbon dioxide emissions spew from power plants, double the amount that comes from ground transportation. Moreover, natural gas is a wonderful complement to wind as a power source. Wind power can be intermittent. That requires a backup fuel supply that can be switched on instantly when the wind dies and switched off just as quickly when it starts blowing again. Natural gas is the only fuel capable of performing that task.

Clearly, natural gas has a prominent role to play in America's energy mix. But whether it's capable of truly freeing the country from dependence on foreign fuel suppliers and whether it will ever be that much cheaper than oil, well, the answers to those questions remain as murky as a gallon of crude.

10

Natural Gas Will Reduce U.S. Dependence on Foreign Oil

The Pickens Plan

T. Boone Pickens was a corporate raider in the 1980s, buying and breaking up many independent oil companies. In 1986 he started and funded a nonprofit organization called the United Shareholders Association to fund a newspaper informing shareholders of corporate abuses. In 1987 he wrote the best-selling book Boone.

America's dependence on foreign oil carries many security risks, and while renewable energies are the ultimate goal, it will take many years to produce them in large enough quantities to satisfy consumers. Natural gas can bridge that transition, and in conjunction with building a modern power grid and giving incentives to homeowners to conserve energy, it will make the United States less dependent on oil imports and also curb greenhouse gas emissions.

America is addicted to foreign oil.

It's an addiction that threatens our economy, our environment and our national security. It touches every part of our daily lives and ties our hands as a nation and as a people.

The addiction has worsened for decades and now it's reached a point of crisis.

In 1970, we imported 24 percent of our oil. Today, it's more than 65 percent and growing.

"America Is Addicted to Foreign Oil," PickensPlan.com, 2009. Copyright © 2009 PickensPlan.com. All Rights Reserved. Reproduced by permission.

Oil prices have come down from the staggering highs of last summer [2008], but lower prices have not reduced our dependence on foreign oil or lessened the risks to either our economy or our security.

If we are depending on foreign sources for nearly two-thirds of our oil, we are in a precarious position in an unpredictable world.

Security Risks

In additional to putting our security in the hands of potentially unfriendly and unstable foreign nations, we spent $475 billion on foreign oil in 2008 alone. That's money taken out of our economy and sent to foreign nations, and it will continue to drain the life from our economy for as long as we fail to stop the bleeding.

Projected over the next 10 years the cost will be $10 trillion—it will be the greatest transfer of wealth in the history of mankind.

Can't we import more oil?

America uses a lot of oil. Every day 85 million barrels of oil are produced around the world. And 21 million of those are used here in the United States.

That's 25 percent of the world's oil demand. Used by just 4 percent of the world's population.

Can't we just produce more oil?

Consider this: America imports 12 million barrels a day, and Saudi Arabia only produces 9 million a day. Is there really more undiscovered oil here than in all of Saudi Arabia?

World oil production peaked in 2005. Despite growing demand and an unprecedented increase in prices, oil production has fallen over the last three years. Oil is getting more expensive to produce, harder to find and there just isn't enough of it to keep up with demand.

The simple truth is that cheap and easy oil is gone.

All Americans are feeling the effects of the recession. And addressing the economy is the top priority of our nation. This is more than bailing out a bank, an insurance firm or a car company. The American economy is huge and has many facets.

The Economic Crisis

To make a real and lasting impact we must seek to do more than create new jobs and opportunities. [T]oday, we must build the platform on which our economy can continue to grow for decades to come.

There is nothing more important to the present and future of our economy than energy. Any effort to address our economic problems will require a thorough understanding of this issue and willingness to confront our dependence on foreign oil and what domestic resources we can use.

While dependence on foreign oil is a critical concern, it is not a problem that can be solved in isolation.

It is a crisis too large to be addressed piecemeal. We need a plan of action on scale with the problems we face. That is the spirit in which the Pickens Plan was conceived. The Pickens Plan is a collection of coordinated steps that together form a comprehensive approach to America's energy needs.

The Pickens Plan

There are several pillars to the Pickens Plan:

- Create millions of new jobs by building out the capacity to generate up to 22 percent of our electricity from wind. And adding to that with additional solar generation capacity

- Building a 21st-century backbone electrical transmission grid

- Providing incentives for homeowners and the owners of commercial buildings to upgrade their insulation and other energy saving options, and

- Using America's natural gas to replace imported oil as a transportation fuel in addition to its other uses in power generation, chemicals, etc.

While dependence on foreign oil is a critical concern, it is not a problem that can be solved in isolation. We have to think about energy as a whole, and that begins by considering our energy alternatives and thinking about how we will fuel our world in the next 10 to 20 years and beyond.

New Jobs from Renewable Energy and Conservation

Any discussion of alternatives should begin with the 2007 Department of Energy study showing that building out our wind capacity in the Great Plains—from northern Texas to the Canadian border—would produce 138,000 new jobs in the first year, and more than 3.4 million new jobs over a 10-year period, while also producing as much as 20 percent of our needed electricity.

Building out solar energy in the Southwest from western Texas to California would add to the boom of new jobs and provide more of our growing electrical needs—doing so through economically viable, clean, renewable sources.

To move that electricity from where it is being produced to where it is needed will require an upgrade to our national electric grid. A 21st-century transmission grid which will, as technology continues to develop, deliver power where it is needed, when it is needed, in the direction that it is needed, will be the modern equivalent of building the Interstate Highway System in the 1950s.

Beyond that, tremendous improvements in electricity use can be made by creating incentives for owners of homes and commercial buildings to retrofit their spaces with proper insulation. Studies show that a significant upgrading of insulation would save the equivalent of one million barrels of oil per day in energy by cutting down on both air conditioning costs in warm weather and heating costs in winter.

A Domestic Fuel

Conserving and harnessing renewable forms of electricity not only has incredible economic benefits, but is also a crucial piece of the oil dependence puzzle. We should continue to pursue the promise of electric or hydrogen powered vehicles, but America needs to address transportation fuel today. Fortunately, we are blessed with an abundance of clean, cheap, domestic natural gas.

Currently, domestic natural gas is primarily used to generate electricity. It has the advantage of being cheap and significantly cleaner than coal, but this is not the only use of our natural gas resources.

Natural gas is not a permanent or complete solution to imported oil.

By aggressively moving to shift America's car, light duty and heavy truck fleets from imported gasoline and diesel to domestic natural gas, we can lower our need for foreign oil— helping President [Barack] Obama reach his goal of zero oil imports from the Middle East within 10 years.

Nearly 20 percent of every barrel of oil we import is used by 18-wheelers moving goods around and across the country by burning imported diesel. An over-the-road truck cannot be moved using current battery technology. Fleet vehicles like buses, taxis, express delivery trucks, and municipal and utility vehicles (any vehicle [that] returns to the "barn" each night where refueling is a simple matter) should be replaced by vehicles running on clean, cheap, domestic natural gas rather than imported gasoline or diesel fuel.

A Comprehensive Plan

Natural gas is not a permanent or complete solution to imported oil. It is a bridge fuel to slash our oil dependence while buying us time to develop new technologies that will ultimately replace fossil transportation fuels. Natural gas is the critical puzzle piece that will help us to keep more of the $350 [billion] to $450 billion we spend on imported oil every year at home, where it can power our economy and pay for our investments in wind energy, a smart grid and energy efficiency.

It is this connection that makes the Pickens Plan not just a collection of good ideas, but a plan. By investing in renewable energy and conservation . . . . [d]eveloping new alternative energies while utilizing natural gas for transportation and energy generation; securing our economy by reducing our dependence on foreign oil; and keeping more money at home to pay for the whole thing[, we can create millions of new jobs].

The Pickens Plan is a bridge to the future—a blueprint to reduce foreign oil dependence by harnessing domestic energy alternatives, and to buy us time to develop even greater new technologies.

Building new wind generation facilities, conserving energy and increasing the use of our natural gas resources can replace more than one third of our foreign oil imports in 10 years. But it will take leadership.

We're organizing behind the Pickens Plan now to ensure our voices will be heard.

Together with President Obama and the Congress, we can take down the old barriers and provide energy security for generations to come, while helping to dig us out of the recession we are in today.

As the President has said, "Yes, we can." And together, as never before, we will.

11

Natural Gas Provides
Clean Energy

Natural Gas Supply Association

The Natural Gas Supply Association represents suppliers of natural gas and encourages the use of natural gas as part of a balanced national energy policy.

Natural gas is found in abundance in the United States. It produces less greenhouse gas emissions than oil or coal and marks an important step toward a healthier environment. Natural gas is not only important to replace coal; given the implementation of proper technologies, it could also fuel cars and public transportation to cut down on smog and acid rain.

Natural gas is an extremely important source of energy for reducing pollution and maintaining a clean and healthy environment. In addition to being a domestically abundant and secure source of energy, the use of natural gas also offers a number of environmental benefits over other sources of energy, particularly other fossil fuels. . . .

Emissions from the Combustion of Natural Gas

Natural gas is the cleanest of all the fossil fuels. Composed primarily of methane, [natural gas has mainly carbon dioxide and water vapor as byproducts of its combustion. Those are] the same compounds we exhale when we breathe. Coal and oil are composed of much more complex molecules, with a higher carbon ratio and higher nitrogen and sulfur contents. This means that when combusted, coal and oil release higher levels of harmful emissions, including a higher ratio of carbon emissions, nitrogen oxides (NO_x), and sulfur dioxide (SO_2). Coal and fuel oil also release ash particles into the environment, substances that do not burn but instead are carried into the atmosphere and contribute to pollution. The combustion of natural gas, on the other hand, releases very small amounts of sulfur dioxide and nitrogen oxides, virtually no ash or particulate matter, and lower levels of carbon dioxide, carbon monoxide, and other reactive hydrocarbons.

The use of fossil fuels for energy contributes to a number of environmental problems. As the cleanest of the fossil fuels, natural gas can be used in many ways to help reduce the emissions of pollutants into the atmosphere. Burning natural gas in the place of other fossil fuels emits fewer harmful pollutants into the atmosphere, and an increased reliance on natural gas can potentially reduce the emission of many of these most harmful pollutants.

The reduction of greenhouse gas emissions has become a primary focus of environmental programs in countries around the world.

Pollutants emitted in the United States, particularly from the combustion of fossil fuels, have led to the development of many pressing environmental problems. Natural gas, [which emits] fewer harmful chemicals into the atmosphere than other fossil fuels, can help to mitigate some of these environmental issues.

Greenhouse Gas Emissions

Global warming, or the greenhouse effect, is an environmental issue that deals with the potential for global climate change due to increased levels of atmospheric greenhouse gases. There are certain gases in our atmosphere that serve to regulate the amount of heat that is kept close to the Earth's surface. Scientists theorize that an increase in these greenhouse gases will translate into increased temperatures around the globe, which would result in many disastrous environmental effects. In fact, the Intergovernmental Panel on Climate Change (IPCC) predicts in its 'Third Assessment Report', released in February 2001, that over the next 100 years, global average temperatures will rise by between 2.4 and 10.4 degrees Fahrenheit.

The principal greenhouse gases include water vapor, carbon dioxide, methane, nitrogen oxides, and some engineered chemicals such as chlorofluorocarbons. While most of these gases occur in the atmosphere naturally, levels have been increasing due to the widespread burning of fossil fuels by growing human populations. The reduction of greenhouse gas emissions has become a primary focus of environmental programs in countries around the world.

The use of natural gas does not contribute significantly to smog formation.

One of the principal greenhouse gases is carbon dioxide. Although carbon dioxide does not trap heat as effectively as other greenhouse gases (making it a less potent greenhouse gas), the sheer volume of carbon dioxide emissions into the atmosphere is very high, particularly from the burning of fossil fuels. In fact, according to the EIA [Energy Information Administration] in its report 'Emissions of Greenhouse Gases in the United States 2000', 81.2 percent of greenhouse gas emissions in the United States in 2000 came from carbon dioxide directly attributable to the combustion of fossil fuels.

Because carbon dioxide makes up such a high proportion of U.S. greenhouse gas emissions, reducing carbon dioxide emissions can play a huge role in combating the greenhouse effect and global warming. The combustion of natural gas emits almost 30 percent less carbon dioxide than oil, and just under 45 percent less carbon dioxide than coal.

The Methane Challenge

One issue that has arisen with respect to natural gas and the greenhouse effect is the fact that methane, the principal component of natural gas, is itself a very potent greenhouse gas. In fact, methane has an ability to trap heat almost 21 times more effectively than carbon dioxide. According to the Energy Information Administration, although methane emissions account for only 1.1 percent of total U.S. greenhouse gas emissions, they account for 8.5 percent of the greenhouse gas emissions based on global warming potential. Sources of methane emissions in the U.S. include the waste management and operations industry, the agricultural industry, as well as leaks and emissions from the oil and gas industry itself. A major study performed by the Environmental Protection Agency (EPA) and the Gas Research Institute (GRI) in 1997 sought to discover whether the reduction in carbon dioxide emissions from increased natural gas use would be offset by a possible increased level of methane emissions. The study concluded that the reduction in emissions from increased natural gas use strongly outweighs the detrimental effects of increased methane emissions. Thus the increased use of natural gas in the place of other, dirtier fossil fuels can serve to lessen the emission of greenhouse gases in the United States.

Smog, Air Quality, and Acid Rain

Smog and poor air quality is a pressing environmental problem, particularly for large metropolitan cities. Smog, the primary constituent of which is ground level ozone, is formed by a chemical reaction of carbon monoxide, nitrogen oxides, volatile organic compounds, and heat from sunlight. As well as creating that familiar smoggy haze commonly found surrounding large cities, particularly in the summertime, smog and ground level ozone can contribute to respiratory problems ranging from temporary discomfort to long-lasting, permanent lung damage. Pollutants contributing to smog come from a variety of sources, including vehicle emissions, smokestack emissions, paints, and solvents. Because the reaction to create smog requires heat, smog problems are the worst in the summertime.

The use of natural gas does not contribute significantly to smog formation, as it emits low levels of nitrogen oxides, and virtually no particulate matter. For this reason, it can be used to help combat smog formation in those areas where ground level air quality is poor. The main sources of nitrogen oxides are electric utilities, motor vehicles, and industrial plants. Increased natural gas use in the electric generation sector, a shift to cleaner natural gas vehicles, or increased industrial natural gas use could all serve to combat smog production, especially in urban centers, where it is needed the most. Particularly in the summertime, when natural gas demand is lowest and smog problems are the greatest, industrial plants and electric generators could use natural gas to fuel their operations instead of other, more polluting fossil fuels. This would effectively reduce the emissions of smog-causing chemicals and result in clearer, healthier air around urban centers. For instance, a 1995 study by the Coalition for Gas-Based Environmental Solutions found that in the Northeast, smog and ozone-causing emissions could be reduced by 50 [percent] to 70 percent through the seasonal switching to natural gas by electric generators and industrial installations.

Particulate emissions also cause the degradation of air quality in the United States. These particulates can include soot, ash, metals, and other airborne particles. A study by the Union of Concerned Scientists in 1998, entitled 'Cars and Trucks and Air Pollution', showed that the risk of premature death for residents in areas with high airborne particulate matter was 26 percent greater than for those in areas with low particulate levels. Natural gas emits virtually no particulates into the atmosphere: in fact, emissions of particulates from natural gas combustion are 90 percent lower than from the combustion of oil, and 99 percent lower than burning coal. Thus increased natural gas use in place of other dirtier hydrocarbons can help to reduce particulate emissions in the U.S.

Acid rain is another environmental problem that affects much of the eastern United States, damaging crops, forests, wildlife populations, and causing respiratory and other illnesses in humans. Acid rain is formed when sulfur dioxide and nitrogen oxides react with water vapor and other chemicals in the presence of sunlight to form various acidic compounds in the air. The principal source of acid rain–causing pollutants, sulfur dioxide and nitrogen oxides, are coal-fired power plants. [As] natural gas emits virtually no sulfur dioxide, and up to 80 percent less nitrogen oxides than the combustion of coal, increased use of natural gas could provide for fewer acid rain–causing emissions.

Industrial and Electric Generation Emissions

Pollutant emissions from the industrial sector and electric utilities contribute greatly to environmental problems in the United States. The use of natural gas to power both industrial boilers and processes and the generation of electricity can significantly improve the emissions profiles for these two sectors.

Natural gas is becoming an increasingly important fuel in the generation of electricity. As well as providing an efficient, competitively priced fuel for the generation of electricity, the increased use of natural gas allows for . . . improvement in the emissions profile of the electric generation industry. According to the National Environmental Trust (NET) in their 2002 publication entitled 'Cleaning Up Air Pollution from America's Power Plants,' power plants in the U.S. account for 67 percent of sulfur dioxide emissions, 40 percent of carbon dioxide emissions, 25 percent of nitrogen oxide emissions, and 34 percent of mercury emissions. Coal-fired power plants are the greatest contributors to these types of emissions. In fact, only 3 percent of sulfur dioxide emissions, 5 percent of carbon dioxide emissions, 2 percent of nitrogen oxide emissions, and 1 percent of mercury emissions come from noncoal-fired power plants. . . .

Natural Gas Vehicles

The transportation sector (particularly cars, trucks, and buses) is one of the greatest contributors to air pollution in the United States. Emissions from vehicles contribute to smog, low visibility, and various greenhouse gas emissions. According to the Department of Energy (DOE), about half of all air pollution and more than 80 percent of air pollution in cities [is] produced by cars and trucks in the United States.

Natural gas can be used in the transportation sector to cut down on these high levels of pollution from gasoline and diesel powered cars, trucks, and buses. In fact, according to the EPA, compared to traditional vehicles, vehicles operating on compressed natural gas have reductions in carbon monoxide emissions of 90 [percent] to 97 percent, and reductions in carbon dioxide emissions of 25 percent. Nitrogen oxide emissions can be reduced by 35 [percent] to 60 percent, and other non-methane hydrocarbon emissions could be reduced by as much as 50 [percent] to 75 percent. In addition, because of the relatively simple makeup of natural gas in comparison to traditional vehicle fuels, there are fewer toxic and carcinogenic emissions from natural gas vehicles, and virtually no particulate emissions. Thus the environmentally friendly attributes of natural gas may be used in the transportation sector to reduce air pollution.

Natural gas is the cleanest of the fossil fuels, and thus its many applications can serve to decrease harmful pollution levels from all sectors, particularly when used together with or replacing other fossil fuels. The natural gas industry itself is also committed to ensuring that the process of producing natural gas is as environmentally sound as possible.

12

Natural Gas Is Not an Alternative to Renewable Energy

Urban Renewable Energy

Urban Renewable Energy's services include comprehensive site assessment and solar-power system design to help businesses and homeowners move toward renewable-energy systems.

Natural gas is touted as a clean alternative to oil, but it is, in fact, merely another fossil fuel. In order to become independent from oil and gas imports and reduce smog and pollution, the United States has to invest in renewable energy. Homeowners as well as large companies must not only conserve energy, they must also use technological advances to retrofit buildings to become self-powered through the structures' own clean energy.

Natural gas seems to be the fossil fuel of choice these days. At one point, it was merely a waste product of oil and coal production but now has reached the point of being an essential component to our total energy picture. The recently announced T. Boone Pickens plan is a bold strategy to wean ourselves from foreign oil. It advocates a massive investment in wind power so that we can divert the natural gas used in electricity production to automobile use. His primary motivation seems to be stemming the export of $700 billion of US wealth each year to foreign oil suppliers. Pickens references the fact that 90% of our current natural gas consumption is met by our North American supply. His plan to increase the percentage of renewables in our electricity grid is right on, but the idea that we should use more natural gas (even in the short term) is completely wrong. Domestic fossil fuels are no better than foreign ones, and both are leading us down a road to major economic and environmental troubles.

The price of natural gas, like many commodities, is difficult to predict. A 40%–50% swing up or down from one year to the next is common. Homeowners and businesses need predictable prices to make sound investment decisions as to what sort of heating, cooling, and electrical equipment they should buy. Natural gas had no real value until the 1970s, and prices remained flat for years. In the early 1990s, with natural gas prices still cheap, suppliers encouraged the widespread adoption of gas[-powered] water heaters, gas[-powered] clothing dryers, and forced-air gas furnaces. It is now the single largest source of fuel for our hot-water and space-heating needs. As domestic demand has exploded, so has international consumption of natural gas. As a consequence, the last five years have brought a doubling of its price and even larger increases have been predicted for the coming years. Natural gas is no longer a cheap fuel.

Replacing the Oil Addiction

We now have a situation where we're trying to replace our oil addiction with a natural gas one. Most American homes use natural gas in some way, 22% of our electricity comes from it, we use it to make fertilizer for growing our food, and some want to shift our transportation system to use more of it. Domestic natural gas suppliers are currently pumping everything they can—there is no more local supply growth to be had. We don't import much natural gas because it is costly to transport overseas. Pipelines move the gas to market from domestic fields, but foreign production must be converted to liquified natural gas (LNG) and loaded on specialized cargo ships.

A major shift towards automobile use of natural gas will spike demand for it, at least in the short term, and the Pickens plan doesn't appear to account for how that new demand will be met. Just as oil consumption grew with cheap oil, so has natural gas consumption grown with low prices. With any rise in demand, it will be impossible to meet our future needs without bringing in supplies from overseas. As this is the primary motivation of the Pickens plan, it seems like the cure may be as bad as the disease.

We need to design and retrofit our buildings in a smarter way.

The solution to this dilemma is to improve the energy efficiency of our homes so that we need less energy. Stopping air leaks and super-insulation is the first and most economic step. Once we have high performance structures, a retrofit with better energy systems will be more cost effective. Renewable energy systems such as solar photovoltaics could then meet a building's electricity needs with a smaller up-front cost. Forced-air gas furnaces are fundamentally inefficient, so retrofitting with radiant heating systems would be a valuable move. The radiant heat fuel source could be a combination of geothermal, solar, and natural gas to slash total natural gas use by as much as 75%. Augmenting the radiant heat system with a pellet stove or masonry heater would even further reduce your exposure to rising natural gas prices. The key is to have multiple energy options. Relying on a single fuel source puts your budget at risk to even moderate price escalation.

Alternative Energies Are Key

Our reliance on foreign energy is one of the major problems that we are facing today. T. Boone Pickens is a man who knows energy, and his plan is a great way to bring widespread attention to the fact that the solution is not to be found by drilling more wells. The wind component of the plan and the assessment of the transportation fuel dilemma are completely admirable parts of his plan. Unfortunately, relying on natural gas to power the shift from oil could lead to more of the same energy troubles that we are seeing today. We need to design and retrofit our buildings in a smarter way. Retaining, consuming, and reusing the energy already at the building is where we should focus our attention. Solar energy is a key component to a brighter future. Let's not cloud our minds or environment further by merely shifting our attention to another fossil fuel.

Organizations to Contact

The editors have compiled the following list of organizations concerned with the issues debated in this book. The descriptions are derived from materials provided by the organizations. All have publications or information available for interested readers. The list was compiled on the date of publication of the present volume; the information provided here may change. Readers need to remember that many organizations take several weeks or longer to respond to inquiries.

American Gas Association (AGA)
(202) 824-7000
Web site: www.aga.org

The American Gas Association represents nearly 200 local energy utility companies that deliver natural gas to more than 56 million homes, businesses, and industries throughout the United States. AGA is an advocate for local natural gas utility companies, and it provides a broad range of programs and services for members, marketers, gatherers, international gas companies, and industry associates. It publishes newsletters online and also distributes the *American Gas Magazine.*

Collective Heritage Institute (CHI)
826 Camino de Monte Rey, #A6, Santa Fe, NM   87505
(505) 986-0366 • fax: (505) 986-1644
E-mail: contactus@bioneers.org
Web site: www.bioneers.org

The Collective Heritage Institute conducts education and research in the areas of biodiversity, ecological farming practices, and environmental restoration. Founded in 1990, CHI mounts projects that include the annual Bioneers Conference and the Restorative Development Initiative. News stories and radio shows are available online.

Cook Inletkeeper

PO Box 3269 / 3734 Ben Walters Lane, Homer, AK   99603
(907) 235-4068 • fax: (907) 235-4069
E-mail: keeper@inletkeeper.org
Web site: www.inletkeeper.org

Cook Inletkeeper is a community-based nonprofit organization seeking to protect Alaska's Cook Inlet watershed. The organization reaches out through monitoring and research to
the scientific community, and its education and advocacy efforts enhance responsible policy making and citizen participa-
tion. Newsletters and reports are posted online.

Greenpeace

702 H Street NW, Washington, DC   20001
(202) 462-1177
Web site: www.greenpeace.org

Greenpeace is working to combat some of the most dangerous
threats to the environment, such as global warming, overfish-
ing, toxic pollution, and the destruction of ancient forests, in
a peaceful, nonviolent manner. Greenpeace makes news stories
and educational texts available on its Web site.

Interstate Natural Gas Association of America (INGAA)

10 G Street NE, Washington, DC   20002
(202) 216-5900 • fax: (202) 216-0870
Web site: www.ingaa.org

INGAA is the North American association that represents interstate and interprovincial natural gas pipeline companies
and speaks for the companies that own and operate those
lines. Its Web site provides information on how pipelines are
built and operated, and it also publishes reports on a multitude of subjects relating to natural gas production and consumption.

National Energy Education Development Project (NEED)

8408 Kao Circle, Manassas, VA   20110

(703) 257-1117 • fax: (703) 257-0037
E-mail: info@need.org
Web site: www.need.org

NEED is a national network of students, educators, and leaders in government and industry dedicated to providing comprehensive energy programming. Through hands-on science, math, drama, social science, art, and music, students work with their peers, teachers, family, and community on energy education programs they design themselves. NEED publishes curriculum resources for students and teachers.

National Petrochemical & Refiners Association (NPRA)
1899 L Street NW, Suite 1000, Washington, DC   20036-3896
(202) 457-0480 • Fax: (202) 457-0486
E-mail: info@npradc.org
Web site: www.npradc.org

The National Petrochemical and Refiners Association (NPRA) represents almost 500 companies, including virtually all U.S. petrochemical refiners and manufacturers. Members work to operate their facilities safely and to protect human health and the environment. Newsletters are available online.

Natural Gas Supply Association (NGSA)
805 15th St. NW, Suite 510, Washington, DC   20005
(202) 326-9300
Web site: www.ngsa.org

NGSA represents suppliers that produce and market natural gas. It supports the use of natural gas and promotes the benefits of market competition, which, in its view, ensures reliable and efficient transportation and delivery of natural gas. NGSA publishes fact sheets and reports, available on its Web site.

North Slope Science Initiative (NSSI)
E-mail: John_F_Payne@ak.blm.gov
Web site: www.northslope.org

The North Slope Science Initiative was developed by federal, state, and local governments with trust responsibilities for land and ocean management. It gathers data about the Alaskan North Slope region and makes such data publicly available. The mission of the NSSI is to improve scientific and regulatory understanding of the North Slope ecosystem in the context of energy resources and climate change. Newsletters can be downloaded from its Web site.

Sierra Club

85 Second Street, Second Floor
San Francisco, CA   94105-3441
(415) 977-5500 • Fax: (415) 977-5799
E-mail: information@sierraclub.org
Web site: www.sierraclub.org

The Sierra Club is a nonprofit, member-supported, public-interest organization that promotes conservation of the natural environment by influencing public policy decisions. News stories and educational materials are available through its Web site.

United States Geological Survey (USGS) Earthquake Hazards Program

USGS National Center, Reston, VA   20192
(703) 648-4000
Web site: www.earthquake.usgs.gov

The USGS provides scientific information to describe and understand the Earth; to minimize loss of life and property from natural disasters; to manage water, biological, energy, and mineral resources; and to enhance and protect quality of life. The USGS maintains the Earth Science Library and provides podcasts on its Web site.

Worldwatch Institute

1776 Massachusetts Ave. NW, Washington, DC   20036-1904
(202) 452-1999 • fax: (202) 296-7365

E-mail: worldwatch@worldwatch.org
Web site: www.worldwatch.org

Worldwatch is a nonprofit, public policy research organization dedicated to informing policy makers and the public about emerging global problems and trends and about the complex links between the world economy and its environmental support systems. Numerous publications are available on its Web site.

Bibliography

Books

Alaska
Department of
Natural Resources

Alaska Oil & Gas Report, Anchorage, AK: Division of Oil and Gas, December 2003.

Alyeska Pipeline
Service Co.

Alyeska: A 30-Year Journey. Alyeska Pipeline Service Co., 2007.

Walter Borneman

Alaska: Saga of a Bold Land. New York, NY: HarperCollins, 2004.

Terrence Cole

Blinded by Riches: The Permanent Funding Problem and the Prudhoe Bay Effect. Anchorage, AK: Institute of Social and Economic Research, University of Alaska Anchorage, 2004.

Kirk Dombrowski

Against Culture: Development, Politics, and Religion in Indian Alaska, Lincoln, NE: University of Nebraska Press, 2001.

David L.
Goodstein

Out of Gas: The End of the Age of Oil. New York: W.W. Norton, 2005.

Stephen Haycox

Alaska: An American Colony. Seattle, WA: University of Washington Press, 2006.

Stephen Haycox
and Mary
Childers
Mangusso, eds.

Frigid Embrace: Politics, Economics, and the Environment in Alaska. Corvallis, OR: Oregon State University Press, 2002.

Kaylene Johnson *Sarah: How a Hockey Mom Turned the Political Establishment Upside Down.* Kenmore, WA: Epicenter Press, 2008.

Joe LaRocca *Alaska Agonistes: The Age of Petroleum: How Big Oil Bought Alaska.* Gloucester City, NJ: Rare Books, 2003.

Saeid Mokhatab, William A. Poe, and James Speight *Handbook of Natural Gas Transmission and Processing,* 1st ed. Oxford, UK: Gulf Professional Publishing, 2006.

National Research Council *Cumulative Environmental Effects of Oil and Gas Activities on Alaska's North Slope.* Washington, DC: The National Academies Press, 2003.

Daniel Nelson *Northern Landscapes: The Struggle for Wilderness Alaska.* Washington, DC: Resources for the Future, 2004.

Bill Richardson *Leading by Example: How We Can Inspire an Energy and Security Revolution.* Hoboken, NJ: Wiley, 2008.

David Sandalow *Freedom from Oil: How the Next President Can End the United States' Oil Addiction.* New York, NY: McGraw-Hill, 2007.

Harold Hilton Stowell *Geology of Southeast Alaska: Rock and Ice in Motion.* Anchorage, AK: University of Alaska Press, 2006.

Periodicals

Alyeska Pipeline Service Co.
"Pipeline Facts: Valdez Marine Terminal," Alyeska-pipe.com, March 30, 2009.

Anchorage Daily News
"Running Conoco," February 1, 2004.

Amanda Bohman
"Trans-Alaska Oil Pipeline Shut Down for Maintenance," *Fairbanks Daily News-Miner*, July 19, 2009.

Kristine Carber
"Scanning the Alaska Pipeline," *Point of Beginning*, December 1, 2006.

Rena Delbridge
"Alyeska Pipeline Retooling as North Slope Oil Production Declines," *Fairbanks Daily News-Miner*, April 27, 2009.

Rena Delbridge
"BP Begins Development of Liberty Oil Field Project on North Slope," *Fairbanks Daily News-Miner*, July 14, 2008.

Evening Standard
"Alaska Vows to Tighten Controls on BP," July 20, 2006.

Charles Homans
"State of Dependence: Ted Stevens's Alaska Problem—And Ours," *Washington Monthly*, November 2007.

Kevin Hostler
"Offshore Work Is Essential for Pipeline's Future," *Fairbanks Daily News-Miner*, April 10, 2009.

Brad Knickerbocker	"Leak Is Latest of Alaska's Pipeline Woes," *Christian Science Monitor*, August 9, 2006.
London Times	"A Drunk, a Gun and a Pipeline with a Hole," April 9, 2004.
Mike McMillan	"Wildfire Overruns Alaska Pipeline at the Yukon Crossing," Smokejumpers.com, December 5, 2004.
National Energy Technology Laboratory	"Fossil Energy—Trans-Alaska Pipeline System," Arctic Energy Office, 2009.
Kristen Nelson	"Kuparuk Anniversary," *Petroleum News*, January 27, 2007.
Steve Quinn	"BP Completes Transit Pipeline Replacement at Prudhoe Bay," *Fairbanks Daily News-Miner*, January 31, 2009.
Stephen Spruiell	"Highway (and Other) Robbery: When It Comes to Raking in the Funds, No One Beats Alaska," *National Review*, November 7, 2005.
Pamela Stern	"Hunting for Hydrocarbons: Representations of Indigeneity in Reporting on the New Mackenzie Valley Gas Pipeline," *American Review of Canadian Studies*, 2007.
Sam Howe Verhovek	"Oil Spill Estimate Increased for Pipeline Leak in Alaska," *Los Angeles Times*, March 11, 2006.

Washington Times   "Arctic Oil, Gas Kept on Hold by
Lawsuits, Economy," July 4, 2009.

Washington Times   "Alaska Pipeline Troubles Have Little
Effect on Prices," August 9, 2006.

Washington Times   "A Natural Gas Crisis," October 14,
2005.

Index